THE SUCCESSFUL THINKER

Laura, You are one of my favorite people! Here's to you! Corey

By

Corey W. Jahnke

Motivational Press®
LEADERS IN GLOBAL PUBLISHING

Published by Motivational Press, Inc.
1777 Aurora Road
Melbourne, Florida, 32935
www.MotivationalPress.com

Manufactured in the United States of America.

ISBN: 978-1-62865-176-8

Contents

"We cannot solve our problems with the same thinking we used when we created them."

Albert Einstein

Chapter One

The Evaluation

In one sentence, her entire world had been blown apart. "Cynthia you have a thirty-two percent employee approval rating." She was in mild shock. *How could this be true?* she thought.

Cynthia was on her way to the corporate office. She was a performer. Her stores always had above average sales and were performing great.

She had always done her best to communicate her expectations to her market. Who cares if the employee approval ratings are weak? The stores made money! *These employees just don't understand what it takes to make the numbers,* she thought to herself.

Cynthia was sure the news was about to get better as Rick would have to share her stores' sales numbers which were certainly more important than a few disgruntled employees. She instantly dismissed this thirty-two percent number and waited for the good news.

The next sentence was worse. "Cynthia, I expect a great deal more than that from my pharmacy district managers," Rick, her boss, exclaimed in a calm, yet disapproving tone.

"Do you realize that your fifteen stores make up fifteen percent of my region? In other words, almost fifteen percent of the people in my region disapprove of their management team.

Store sales may be temporarily up due to marketing and other economic factors, but over the long haul, do you realize how serious and permanent employee ratings are? Do you understand how this relates to the individual employees? Their families? Their kids?"

Rick dropped this bomb coldly and without fanfare. He waited in silence for a response.

She had no response.

One year ago, Cynthia Meyer had moved to Milwaukee, Wisconsin from Casper, Wyoming to open up four new stores, take over a region and build her internal resume.

A very process-oriented individual, Cynthia Meyer thought she was on a steady rise to eventually become a VP at the corporate offices in San Diego.

Her family was supportive of the move. The past four years as a manager of the store in Wyoming had given her the experience she needed to move from store management to leading a group of stores.

Rick's admonishment of her performance came as a complete shock.

When she first moved to Milwaukee, she thought, *in two more years, I'll have* this *guy's job.* But now, even with her best effort she was being thanked with a slap in the face from the very people who worked for her.

After an uncomfortable few moments of dead silence, she composed herself enough to weakly stammer out the words, "I'm sorry, Rick. Certainly, the sales figures show..." Rick cut her off.

"Cynthia, same store sales are an important driver of performance, but when it comes to leadership, it is only one of dozens of metrics. Managing a store is not the same as leading a team of stores."

He was about to continue on, but a distant memory instantly flashed in his mind.

It wasn't long ago that he was on the other side of this table. Eleven years in four separate districts, Rick had taken his skills and experience and was now head of over half of the company's retail stores.

He reflected on a day, not so many years ago, when he had a similar discussion with his boss.

If it weren't for his "secret" mentor, Rick probably would have been canned a while ago. He had no idea of the huge gaff he had made. If it weren't for a chance meeting with his mentor, his life would have turned out quite differently.

His mistake was not an event—it was a style, it was a belief, it was an inferior pattern of thinking.

And it was almost identical to Cynthia's.

Now, as Cynthia's boss, he was one sentence away from crushing her and turning her world upside down.

Like his review seven years ago, Rick knew she hadn't seen this coming either. His boss had given him a second chance. Why shouldn't he do the same? Would it be possible that Cynthia could benefit from a mentor who could teach her, as his mentor had done, how to become a successful thinker? Was she open to change?

It was in this instant that his plan to fire her flipped to doing something unheard of. Cynthia had no idea how close she had come to starting over again.

He put his hands on his desk. "Listen," he said. "I've got an idea. The fiscal year ends in about twelve weeks and I am going to do something a bit unconventional.

At the beginning of the new fiscal year, I'm going to add an additional store to your roster that is about two hours north of where you live right now. It'll be a bit of a hike, but I promise you it'll be worth it."

Still in shock over Rick's earlier comment, all she heard was "two hours north" and thought that she had been banished to the Siberia of the Midwest. Her brain reached out to recall what her ears had heard, but not deciphered.

Still reeling from Rick's previous comments, she rewound the tape in her head and realized she was not being fired. Cynthia's confidence and ego came back into focus. *Perhaps this additional store so far north needs someone like me,* she thought.

Perhaps adding the store to her district was Rick's way of aligning her style of management with a store that would appreciate her and not give her bad ratings like the other ones. *Maybe this store needs me,* she thought.

She had no idea that the exact opposite was true. It wasn't the store that needed her—it was Cynthia that needed this store. Or rather, one particular employee who worked there.

Cynthia collected her thoughts. Her heart was beating like a locomotive inside her chest two minutes earlier with Rick's criticism and her very real apprehension about being let go.

Almost within the same breath, Rick was giving more responsibility. A new store to manage! Was this a test? Was he giving her a store to manage and improve or a black sheep to seal the deal on her termination?

She had known Rick to be an experienced man who knew what he was doing. This wasn't a test or a Machiavellian plan for a clean termination. Cynthia set aside her doubts and suspicions and waited as Rick filled in the rest of the confusing statement.

This was something else.

"Let me explain," Rick said. "There is a guy at that new store, and I think he might be just the thing you'll need in this district. Once you meet him—well, trust me. You'll be a perfect fit."

A glimmer of hope flashed across Cynthia's face. She leaned forward in her chair and awaited more details. She pictured a young, eager store manager who would benefit from her knowledge and experience.

Her mind instantly went into the future where she would float in, solve their issues and regain her high ratings from her employees.

She pictured a pliable manager who had minions she could mold and manage to match her style.

Rick cracked a smile so small it was undetectable to anyone who didn't know him. Cynthia suspected that Rick wanted to say more.

It was odd. Just two minutes ago, she was sure she was being fired but now, Rick had just given her a new store to regain her ratings and keep her on her track to the corporate office.

Rick was careful not to give away any more details. Of course, he wanted to tell Cynthia that she was going to this store to unlearn some of the beliefs that had affected not just her business performance, but her personal life as well.

He purposefully left out the true meaning of this assignment. He knew the discovery was part of the process and the surprises she was about to experience were part of the journey to reshape her management style and hopefully give her leadership potential.

He was looking for signs from her to see if she would take the initiative. Was she truly open to change? There was only one person Rick knew would be able to determine that in the next few weeks.

Rick's facial expressions were far from telling, especially to Cynthia. Even though she knew he wasn't happy, this latest shift from Rick was confusing and strangely welcomed.

The sword of Damocles had been removed and his quirky behavior now took a back seat to her thoughts on her new assignment.

Rick sighed before he began speaking again. His plan now in play, he needed to also give her the consequences of any inability to adapt.

He never wanted his employees to feel intimidated by him or feel undo pressure. At the same time, he was concerned about the future of the company and his own job security.

Regardless of how this experiment turned out, there is a consequence to success as well as failure. While he couldn't disclose the consequences of Cynthia's potential success, he had to let her know what would happen if she failed.

"Cynthia, the company can't tolerate ratings like this two years in a row. You've got a little time to turn things around, but when we meet for your next review, if the results are the same, the conversation will be different... and not in a good way."

Cynthia slowly shook her head in agreement, but didn't say anything. She signed her evaluation form and quickly moved to exit the room, anxious to try to digest all that had happened.

She felt numb inside. She knew she had never been a great "connector," but thirty-two percent? Did this mean her employees hated her? They didn't know how hard she worked! What was their issue? Would this new store be easier to work with?

She had just moved her family half way across the country. They had no connections or network. This job was their foundation. Without it, they would be lost. Without this job, her family would be in serious trouble. What was she going to do? She couldn't afford to lose this job.

Her family was already underwater financially as they struggled to keep up with daily expenses. Ask anyone who earns less than they spend and struggles to get by and you'll get similar answers. It's never one thing, but a combination of things that create the constant financial stress.

Her husband, Don, had recently left his job in Casper. Cynthia's promotion to manage the stores in Wisconsin came with a modest increase in pay. But, it wasn't close to matching Don's previous salary.

With Don acting as a "house husband," they didn't need day care for the kids anymore and that helped a little bit, but it didn't even offset his night school expenses.

What made the situation especially delicate was they hadn't taken into account the drastically higher cost of living in Milwaukee, as compared to their small town life in Casper, Wyoming.

The twenty pounds she had put on over the past year, which she blamed on meetings and fast food, had forced her to buy new clothes that she couldn't afford.

In fact, she wouldn't have even liked those clothes if they were in her old size. But she felt the need to buy them so that she could fit in and feel like a "big city" executive.

To add insult to injury, the travel demands and other stresses of the job had put a strain on her relationship with Don, as well as their three children.

Her seven-year-old son, Jared, had gotten into trouble the first week of school and Tommy, the five-year-old was acting out abruptly and more anti-socially than other kids his age.

Monica, their eldest, was becoming a teenager and also required additional attention and time. But both were in short supply.

Don did the best he could, but the changes were clear. Her family life had deteriorated and now she had almost lost the only thing that had kept them together—her job. She wondered if she was losing control over her entire world.

As she was going out of her conference with Rick, Angela was going in. All of the district managers were getting their evaluations as the "closing act" of the regional meeting.

She quietly said to Angela, "I'll meet you at the Starbucks across the street."

She really felt like driving away to anywhere else as fast as she could. That, however, was not possible, because Angela was her ride home.

Chapter Two

The Ride Home

After what seemed like forever, Angela came bouncing into Starbucks, jiggling her car keys in front of her face. Before Angela could say anything, Cynthia could glean a lot simply from how she looked. She wasn't dragging in with a sad expression. She wasn't storming in as though someone had done her wrong. And she didn't appear to have any tears streaming down her face. With a smiling face full of happiness, she said, "Let's roll!"

It was clear that Angela's experience with Rick went better than Cynthia's. Like Cynthia, Angela had come from a small town in the Western states. Her roots, upbringing and experience were quite similar to Cynthia's, which was one reason they got along.

Angela had been in the pharmacy business about the same number of years as Cynthia, was married with two kids and loved the outdoors like Cynthia.

The only difference, it seemed, was that Angela didn't appear to worry as much. She never mentioned climbing the corporate ladder and rarely talked about her store's numbers.

In fact, whenever Cynthia did ask about her numbers, Angela would answer, but always follow up with a smile and some comment about an employee's birthday or the graduation party for the child of a customer.

To her credit, Angela was intuitive, she had gotten the sense that Cynthia meeting was less than stellar. She wanted to say something to comfort Cynthia but was having trouble holding back the positive emotions she was experiencing. Her evaluation had been outstanding.

Cynthia was experiencing an upset stomach, she was hunched over, eyes bulging out of their sockets, and she really struggled with the dryness she seemed to be experiencing in her throat.

Angela's giddiness was infectious. It even caught the attention of some of the other shop patrons, if not the baristas themselves.

She tried hard not to overdo it, but she had, in fact, done very well. It was her charisma and the way she looked at a person that made everyone instantly like her.

As they pulled out of town set for the three-hour drive north, Cynthia stared out the window wondering how things had gotten so bleak in what seemed like a blink of an eye.

She did what many people do when faced with such a predicament. She started comparing herself to Angela.

Angela, on the other hand, quietly decided to "give Cynthia some space".

After they had gone about 30 miles, Cynthia realized that she could bear the silence no longer.

She blurted out what Angela would surely not have expected: "Rick told me that I stink at my job, that my employees hate me and all that he can do for me is put an additional store, two hours away, in my district."

Angela, sensing the state of confusion and sadness Cynthia was feeling, sought to console her. She reached out her right hand and placed it on top of Cynthia's left hand as she began talking again.

"I'm toast! Maybe I should have applied for a job at Starbucks," and her voice tailed off into a quiet sob.

But Angela had been there before, and she knew what it felt like to fall on hard times. It was actually a bit of a disappointment to her when she learned from Rick that one of her favorite stores was the result of carefully crafted redistricting.

But Rick assured her that allowing for this change to take place would mean an increase in responsibility. She would be "graduating," Rick said.

And for that, Angela was truly grateful. It proceeded to give her the confidence to know that she was on the right track with respect to the company, her stores and her employees.

Upon learning that the store would be traded to Cynthia's district, she could understand its importance and necessity.

"Two hours away? Is it north of your district?" Angela asked.

"Yes... how did you know?" asked Cynthia.

"Ah, Otis..." Angela said very thoughtfully, referring to the manager of the store that was now in Cynthia's district.

She flashed a gleeful smile and her eyes sparkled a little. It was clear to Cynthia that Angela held Otis in high regard, though she wasn't exactly sure why.

"Otis?" shot back Cynthia. "Who is Otis? You mean that's what the extra two hour drive and adding a new store is all about? One guy? Like that's going to help!"

Angela chuckled out loud. "I remember five years ago when I thought that as well. I'll never forget confronting him in the bookstore that day. Smartest thing I ever did. I just got another great evaluation because of what he taught me!"

"What?" Cynthia exclaimed as she shook her head. "Let me get this straight; I'm *supposed* to go to him for help?" She closed her eyes for a minute so that she could fully process the notion of this younger guy with less experience making a huge enough difference in her performance that she is suddenly a star, like her counterpart copilot, Angela. "He's going to be working for me. How is that even logical?"

Angela laughed harder than before. "Cynthia, you *are* supposed to go to him for help. But, make no mistake about it, he won't be working for you!"

"No!" Cynthia firmly stated. She couldn't believe what Angela was saying. "Rick said I'm going to be *his* district manager. Of course he'll be working for me!"

"Let me tell you a story," Angela said, shaking her head. "Five years ago, I heard from one of the other employees that Otis was at the bookstore working on his next book. Here's a manager who also fancies himself an author. So, I decided that it was the perfect opportunity to go and give him a piece of my mind.

"Maybe this guy was a snob or brilliant. I didn't know which, but his influence with our employees and management was quietly unmistakable. I was shocked when a senior level VP told me Otis might be able to help 'get me on the right path'.

"It was like the scene in the movie *Ferris Bueller's Day Off*, when the character Charlie Sheen plays suggests to Ferris' sister, 'I know a guy you should talk to.' When I heard it was one of my subordinates, I was livid. When I got there, I went in with a full head of steam ready to... I don't even know what I was ready to, but I was ready to...

"Anyway, there he was, just tapping away on his laptop and I walked up to him. 'You know sometimes I just hate you!' I said to him. 'I'm supposed to be your district manager and you have ten times more influence in my district than I do!'

"He finished typing the sentence he was working on, looks up and very slowly says, 'I know, isn't that fascinating?'

"I was stunned by the straightforward way in which he said it, but it kind of broke the ice because it confirmed that I wasn't imagining things.

"Then I said, 'It has been brought to my attention that if you fully support an initiative, the entire market supports it, but if you don't, it becomes D.O.A.'

"He smiles and says, 'I know, isn't that fascinating?'

"I almost punched him that time!" she said jokingly. "But, I finally came to my senses. I knew that I really needed his help. I just kind of growled at him instead and said, 'Fascinating or not, I—and this part just killed me to have to say—I need your help. I need you to endorse me. What is that going to take?"

"He had this wide smile on his face and he studied me very carefully. I don't know exactly what he was doing. Sizing me up? But I remember being a bit uncomfortable.

"Finally, after what seemed like forever, he said with a very alarming calmness in his voice, 'Okay, Ange, I'll help you. I'll help you... as soon as you start meeting *my* expectations.'"

Cynthia gasped. "He did not say that out loud!"

"Oh, yes, he did!" Angela continued, "Can you believe the nerve of that guy? Then he went on to ask me a really tough question: 'Why do *you* think you have an influence problem?'

"I thought, 'Duh. If I knew that, we wouldn't be talking!' When I looked at him I could tell that wouldn't be the answer he was looking for. I said that I didn't really know. I just knew that whenever I handed down directions from above, no one seemed to act on them until I sent out threatening emails and faxes.

"His next question sucked. 'How often do you do that?' he asked me bluntly. I hated him for that, but I reluctantly answered, 'It seems like that is all I do!'

Then he goes, 'Exactly!' adding, 'How's that workin' for ya?'

"I *really* wanted to punch him then! I've seen the Dr. Phil Show too, ya know? But he was right and I knew it. I had reduced myself from being an influential leader to a major pain in the you-know-what.

"Still, he was a guy—a guy that I believed worked for *me*, and I wasn't about to give him the satisfaction of being right. In fact, the best I could do was to grumble out, 'I *really* do hate you, you know?'

"But, he kind of laughed at me, the way a husband does when he knows he's right. Then suddenly he got all serious with me and says, 'That's okay, someday you won't.

"Someday you will thank me for the following sentence: *Effective* managers see themselves as someone who *works for* their subordinates and, as long as you continue to send expectation after expectation, with no hint that you even have one foot in reality, your people will not 'follow' you because you are not leading anywhere.'"

"He said that out loud as well!" Cynthia exclaimed in disbelief. "Who does he think he is?"

"Oh, it gets better," Angela continued. "He went on to say, 'You have fallen into the trap that says 'passing along direction' is the same as leadership. You must connect with people and communicate, "I understand your problems and concerns" well in advance of "I need you to work on my problems and concerns." This is what leadership means. Does it not?'

"Of course it did!" Angela continued in a sad, humbled tone: "I knew that. I had just let it get away from me. I was embarrassed, so I got up and grabbed my purse. Then I just blurted out, 'I think I hate you even more than I did when I sat down.'

"I had to go somewhere. Anywhere. My head was racing a million miles an hour. As I took my first step away, do you know what he did? He just went back to writing, like dropping all this on me was part of it; part of who he was. I mean, who does that, right?"

Cynthia was like a deer in the headlights. He sounded like an arrogant jerk to her. This was the guy Rick wanted her to manage? Or... actually give advice to her? How could he help her?

Just then, Angela said something she didn't expect. "Suddenly, I realized he had called me Ange! He actually called me Ange! No one calls me Ange!

"I turned around, marched back to the table and before I could give him another piece of my mind, he matter-of-factly looks up and says,

'Listen, Ange, if we are going to be friends, you have to realize that I'm on your side. I want you to succeed. I want your people to succeed. We are not enemies. The relentless drift of events is the enemy. But if we are going to make you successful, you have got to learn to think like successful people think!'

"Then he just goes back to writing as if he had just performed a great oratory and I was the audience and the curtain had gone down. All I could do was stand there. I mean, I wanted to punch him, fire him, or at least walk away.

"It was a very confusing moment. But, the thought kept pounding through my head: Friends? This guy works for me and he's all acting like he thinks he's some sort of mentor or something!

"All of a sudden, he gets up, walks over to the bookstore's coffee shop, and buys two sodas. He walks back and sets one down in front of the chair I was sitting at, but he doesn't say anything. He just goes back to writing.

"I didn't have a clue what to do next, but eventually I sat down."

"What happened next?" Cynthia asked, totally riveted.

"You won't believe me if I told you," Angela stated. "There is no way anyone would believe the changes not just in my evaluations, but something much deeper. In fact, it's probably better you don't hear it from me."

Cynthia's dread deepened, as she wondered what was going to happen next.

Chapter Three

The Law of Contribution

"I have an idea," Angela said with excitement. "I have to be in his store on Friday for inventory prep. I think it's only appropriate that the exiting DM make the introduction for the entering DM, don't you think?

"Why not meet me up there at, say, three p.m., and get it out of the way? You may as well get 'initiated' sooner as opposed to later!" Angela said with a huge smile on her face.

Despite Angela's obvious excitement, Cynthia remained a little uneasy.

Angela was losing a store that Cynthia was picking up. The two-hour drive was going to be tiring enough, but now, with the knowledge that Rick had added this store so she could learn from one of from her employees made no sense to her.

In her mind, major initiatives and programs should be lead by the district manager, not some store employee. Angela made this guy out to be some nut-job guru or Tony Robbins wannabe.

Now, bubbly Angela was excited to turn over part of her territory to her so she could meet Otis. Otis? Was Angela taking part in some elaborate prank?

Cynthia had known Angela for quite some time. They had become instant friends after their first regional meeting. In a lot of ways, they acted like sisters. Even though Cynthia was swimming in her own version of hell, she wanted to believe that there was a light at the end of the tunnel.

Perhaps Angela's introduction to this Otis character had some deeper relevance. Perhaps it was time to open her mind just a crack.

Angela was one of the most highly awarded district mangers in the entire company. She knew her stuff and her people adored her.

And while there was a tiny sliver within Cynthia that was slightly jealous of her friend's success, she knew that Angela wanted her to succeed.

When Friday rolled around, they met in the front of the large department store and began to walk back to the pharmacy area.

They were exchanging small talk about the events of the week when suddenly Cynthia saw a familiar face.

She was a little shocked by what she was seeing. *Phil?* she thought. Phil was one of her pharmacy managers, and he was entering the main aisle with another man.

But then she remembered that Phil had mentioned he would be picking up overtime here while one of this store's regular pharmacists was on vacation.

Phil was dressed in a requisite white lab coat, but the other man was not. The other man had a tie on that had an image of Mickey Mouse on it, and his name tag lanyard had several pins on it. From a distance Cynthia couldn't make out what they were.

The closer they got, however, the more she wondered what was going on. Phil looked like he was visibly upset. The other man looked mildly concerned.

As the two ladies approached, the man with the Mickey Mouse tie looked up and noticed Angela. He then lifted up his hand with a gesture that said very clearly, "I see you, but I need a moment here."

Angela had a feeling Cynthia would benefit from what was about to happen, so she urged Cynthia to move close enough so that she could overhear the conversation. Then she nodded forward with her head, and quietly said: "Otis."

This is Otis? Great! Cynthia thought to herself. *I'm supposed to learn something from the leader of the Mickey Mouse Club!*

She thought for a moment about the image that formed in her mind when Rick was talking about him. She even thought about the one that appeared when Angela was talking about him.

But none of them captured the essence of this person, who seemed to be radiating with light. She was obviously curious about this person's true nature, but for now, she was mesmerized by his physical features.

He appeared to be in very good shape. He wasn't too muscular, but just enough to create sculpting. His bright blue eyes sparkled with enthusiasm, and his posture was upright and erect. A messy crop of blonde hair sat atop his head.

But that did not stop her from drawing disgust from his, well... costume. Attached to Otis' lanyard were Disney character pins: Goofy, Dumbo, Snow White and all seven dwarves.

She was very unimpressed. To her, he looked like a waiter in a restaurant that promoted "flair."

All of my pharmacists dress very professionally, she further thought. She desperately tried to recall the rules in the company handbook, thinking that Otis may be violating several of the physical appearance regulations.

I hope he doesn't have any Disney tattoos, she thought while a grim expression planted itself on her face.

Unaware at a conscious level, Cynthia was not a Disney fan. She never got into "The Happiest Place on Earth" theme. It was not something that piqued her interest.

If she would have given it deep thought (that she had not done in over twenty years) she would have realized her disdain was based on an early desire to go to Disneyland once, just to see it, so she could tell all of her friends that she and her family went on a wonderful vacation.

As hard as she tried to convince her parents to go along with her plan, they had always come up with an excuse. After a while, she just gave up on trying to convince them, and she sulked into a deep sadness.

Since that time, seeing the omnipresent Disney brand plastered on billboards and newspaper ads and television always gave her a bad feeling.

To see those icons of her fractured past on the person who was supposedly going to turn her into a better performer, a better leader, was more than disconcerting—it was a boiling pot of angst about to overflow.

Before she could finish the rest of her private thoughts, Otis said something to Phil that grabbed her attention. "Phil, why are you so upset? What did we do to upset you? I mean, we always have a great time working together. What's going on?"

Phil's response was really interesting: "It's not you, it's Harvey! If he was here, I'd throttle him!"

Otis cocked his head like a dog. He responded in an almost fake sounding confused tone. "Well, you'll have to help me with that one. Harvey is in Florida. And that's why you're here, right?"

Phil answered gruffly, "All I've heard all day long is how great Harvey is, how everybody loves him, and what a great job he does for you! And every time I hear that he's doing so well I just have to shake my head in disbelief.

"I can tell you a different story. When he worked for *me*, he couldn't do anything right. Don't you remember?

"If he wasn't messing up the procedures, he was busy doing other things he wasn't supposed to be doing. I mean, he wasn't getting into a lot of trouble or anything like that. But he was clearly walking around as if he had one screw loose!

"I was constantly going behind him to make sure he was keeping up with everything. And he would always roll his eyes and sulk around like a lonely cat. That's why I asked to have him transferred here!

"Now, so am I to suddenly believe, he is some sort of rock star? Excuse me? That Harvey? Why didn't he put in that kind of effort when he worked for me?"

Otis laughed out loud and said very boldly, "Oh, I see, you're mad because you didn't give him the opportunity to succeed! Harvey doesn't work for me. I work for him!"

"You're not funny, Otis!" Phil shot back. He was obviously not amused.

Cynthia took a moment to think about what she was hearing. In fact, she could recall situations with her own employees where it felt like she just wasn't getting enough out of them.

There was one manager she had to unfortunately "let go" of three months ago after a very heated discussion took place in the manager's office. Apparently, the manager had gotten into an argument with a customer in front of a few of his staff members.

Clearly the manager was at fault, Cynthia had surmised without a thought to the contrary. And, without hearing any of the comments from the witnesses, she called the manager to set up a meeting.

She wouldn't accept any of his excuses. Her job was to manage her people. In her mind, there was no excuse for yelling at a customer.

And with that, she dismissed him of his duties and turned one of the store's underlings as the new interim manager.

Otis put his hand on Phil's shoulder and asked if he could share the story of Jim, the greatest man he had ever known. Phil said, "Whatever." Otis' eyes drifted back to the past as he began his story.

"I grew up in Chicago during Walter Payton's glory years and attended Pharmacy School at the height of Michael Jordan's stardom. Forgive the sports analogy, but at the time, ninety percent of the conversations during this period revolved around hero worship for these great performers," Otis reflected.

"At that time, my dream was to be the guy 'with the ball.' That, lucky for me, was when I ran into Jim Borgetti, who taught me that the guy with the ball is maybe the least important guy on the team."

Phil looked a little confused by Otis' statement. How could Jordan and Payton be the *least* important guys on the team? But he knew that Otis would fill in all the missing pieces.

"I was able to land a summer job as an intern at Consumer's Pharmacy in a small town in Illinois. It was a great opportunity for me to learn the ropes and become familiar with the company. All summer long I watched these two guys, Jim and his partner John, work together.

"John was absolutely dazzling! He was crazy with passion. He was outgoing in a way that left customers spellbound. Borderline cartoon character, comedian and Ritz Carlton concierge. I mean, can you imagine being a customer who was going to pick up a prescription and having to deal with this guy?

"Half the time he left the customers in stitches and feeling as though they were the most important person in John's life. But, most importantly, he made sure everyone had a smile on their face when they left.

"The employees thought John was some sort of god, and the doctors and nurses at the clinic next door thought his pharmacy was *the* place to get prescriptions filled (they told practically every patient to go in and ask for John).

In fact, for two months I worshipped him myself. To be honest, I wanted to be him. And who wouldn't? He just had this excitement about him. It was something that you just couldn't escape. Every day, I loved going to work because I knew that I would have a fascinating and thrilling day.

"As the summer wore on, I began to realize something that started to bother me.

I noticed that things between the two partners were slightly unbalanced. While John was out front getting all of the glory and attention, Jim was in the back putting together the orders as quickly and accurately as humanly possible. Pour, count, label. Pour, count. label. Pour, count, label. Watching him almost made me dizzy.

Obviously, John filled some prescriptions and Jim talked to some patients, but it was easily 80/20 the other way around. I didn't like it. Here poor Jim is working so hard, and John is the one everybody loves.

"Finally, being young and naive, I proudly said to Jim, 'You know, I think it stinks! You do all of the work, and John gets all of the credit!'

"I was sure he would think I was cool for noticing. Well, that was not the case. He looked at me sharply, fire in his eyes, but said nothing. Taking me by the coat, he sat me down in the back room and said something I'll never forget as long as I live.

"'I cannot believe someone as smart as you are has missed the whole point. John has an effect on people that I cannot even begin to understand! *My* job is to do everything in my power to free him up to do what he does best so that the entire team does well.

"When you watch the Bulls tonight, pay attention to how many picks are set for Jordan, and how many set-up passes he gets. Maybe you'll learn something.'

"Twenty years later, I mailed Jim a thank-you letter for giving me a successful career. A few days later, he called me at work. When I told him that story, he didn't even remember saying it."

"So, that's what you do for Harvey. Give him the opportunity to do what he does best!"

Phil said sheepishly, "I feel kind of dumb now."

"Believe me, I know the feeling," Otis agreed. "Now, let's go make Harvey proud and do what we do best!"

The two men shook hands and Phil started back to the pharmacy, still processing the conversation that had just taken place.

Cynthia, still placed strategically within earshot of Otis, took a few moments to study Otis' appearance once more while she soaked in the words he had just spoken. It sounded to her like he was saying something about the power of teamwork, but she wasn't quite getting it.

She looked over to where Angela was standing, beaming yet again, as though she had just attended a motivational seminar and she was reaping the benefits of truly enlightening information.

Otis turned and walked over to the ladies, greeting enthusiastically, "Hey Ange, how's your day going?"

"Well, Otis, I've had a marvelous day. Thanks for asking." She bowed her head slightly when she said that, perhaps to acknowledge the wisdom that Otis possessed, perhaps simply a gesture of polite conversation.

"Which brings me to why I'm here. As you have already learned, your store will be moving into a new district at the beginning of the new fiscal year."

"Yes," Otis said, "I'm actually quite excited about the new opportunities to meet the management staff."

"Well, I'm glad you feel that way," Angela beamed. "As a matter of fact, there's someone I'd like you to meet." She gestured for Cynthia to come closer to her.

Cynthia shyly inched over to where Angela and the glowing young pharmacy manager were standing. "I'd like you to meet Cynthia, your new boss!"

"Oh, it's nice to meet you, Cynthia. I've actually heard..."

Cynthia impulsively blurted out, "You've heard what?"

"Ah, who cares what I've heard. It doesn't matter because this is the first time I'm meeting you in person. And it's quite unfair to create judgments about people before you've even met them. Wouldn't you agree?"

"I... I guess so," Cynthia uttered with a slightly awkward smile. For most of the time she had been at the pharmacy, Cynthia had been absorbing the conversation, analyzing the data and making judgments about Otis, his attire and what that meant or said about him.

How it was possible for a grown man to pull off wearing decorative attire that more closely resembled a carnival worker than a professional at work. How was it that he wore the bling of a five year old, but spoke like a marriage counselor?

But all of judgment was starting to melt away as she learned more about this Otis character standing in front of her. It was as if he possessed all the enthusiasm and inspiration in the world in his strong and caring hands.

"Cynthia," Angela interrupted, "did you know that Otis here is a company Pharmacist of the Year award winner, and that he has a ninety-seven percent employee approval rating?" Angela asked proudly.

It was clear to Cynthia that Angela totally admired Otis and wanted to start the introductions off with a bang.

Wow. Ninety-seven percent. Cynthia thought to herself. *What does he do, buy them cars?*

Otis chimed in so as not to let Angela continue to brag about him, "It's so nice to meet you, my friend. Welcome to the team!"

Apparently, he wasn't all smiles because he suddenly sensed an urgency to get back to what he was doing. "Ange, I really need to get back to the bench. I'm sure our impromptu meeting has put us a little behind." And with that, Otis shot back to the pharmacy.

Otis shook hands with Angela. "It's very nice to meet you, Cynthia," he said as he reached out to meet Cynthia's hand. "I really look forward to working with you. I know it's going to be a blast!"

"Yeah," Cynthia said, not quite finished processing his level of excitement about her.

"The king is heading back to his court," Angela mused to Cynthia loudly enough for Otis to overhear as he was quickly walking away.

More like the joker, thought Cynthia.

Cynthia turned and commented to Angela, "That story, the one about the guy from Chicago, do you think he really operates that way?"

"How do you mean?" Angela asked, drifting back to the person she was with. "Well, I mean Harvey really struggled when he was in our market. How could he turn around so quickly?" Cynthia asked in a bewildered way.

"Come on with me," Angela said as she turned toward the back of the store. "I'll tell you all about it, but first I want to buy something for you. Think of it as a 'Welcome To Otis' House' Warming Gift." Angela was giggling when she said that, and then she took Cynthia to the school supplies aisle.

Cynthia was a little befuddled when Angela picked up a black journal with gold lettering. On the cover page she wrote the words: "The Seven Laws of Leading Effectively in the Twenty-First Century." On the first page she wrote, "Law Number One: The Law of the Contribution."

Chapter Four

The King and His Court

As the two ladies walked over to the cash register area, Cynthia wasn't sure what to think. *Why would Angela be buying me a journal?* she wondered. *And what is this Law of Contribution?*

After Angela paid for the book, she handed it to Cynthia and said proudly, "This is just a little something to start you on your journey. Otis did the same thing for me, and I had the same funny expression when he did it, too!

As I will explain to you, the Law of the Contribution is the first of the seven laws he taught me about how to become an effective leader and a very successful thinker.

"By now you already know, from my telling of the encounter with Otis at the bookstore, that in addition to working in one of our stores, he's also trying to make it as a writer. In fact, he's just as dedicated to writing—if not more so—as he is to serving and helping others reach their full potential.

"Several years ago, while Otis was conducting a bunch of online surveys for a book he was writing, he became fascinated by the responses. He told me that his surveys showed that the top source of job satisfaction was the ability to make a meaningful contribution at work.

Now, think about that for just a minute. Making a meaningful contribution at work ranked number one in qualities that make an employee satisfied with his or her job.

"Well, he began to interview people and realized that people who are older than us, those who worked mainly in the Industrial Age, actually made stuff and could therefore say things like, 'I made the handle for that car door.' There was a tangible result of a person's effort.

If you were working on an assembly line, you could imagine that the tiny part you would play in making putting something together could turn into a source of pride when you see the finished product. Your hands, your time and your work made an impact.

"However, in the Information/Service Age, that's not often the case. In the Information/Service Age, your contributions are not nearly as tangible. You may not be able to see definitively how your talking to someone on the phone or helping a customer find a solution to a problem really makes a difference."

"Yeah, I kind of see where you're going with this," Cynthia said. "As a DM, I don't often see the many ways in which my employees work to assist customers and make sales. And I surely am not around enough to understand how they truly feel while they are working."

Cynthia started to wonder how her employees were really feeling about their jobs, but she was still a bit clueless about how to make a greater effort to reach out to her employees. She listened to Angela with growing interest as she continued.

"Well, here's the solution! Make sure everybody has a space to contribute and make sure everyone knows what their contributions are expected to be. Give them the tools and support they need to succeed. Then lavish them with authentic praise and reward them for the part they play in the team's victories!"

Cynthia thought that was simple enough. As she thought about her employees, she began to wonder if she had been doing that. But as she continued to think about the relationship she had with her employees, she couldn't find anything in her leadership style that would come close to what Angela was describing.

This new method of leading was still a bit foggy, but the results were irrefutable.

"That's what Otis did with Harvey," Angela said. "He gave Harvey a spot on the team and allowed him to contribute and make a meaningful difference. Harvey responded in a powerful way. Consequently, he has increased Harvey's role significantly and Harvey has stepped up. Now he is playing really big!"

"So, by expecting more from Harvey... he has become more?" Cynthia asked, even though she was still not quite able to put two and two together.

"It's more than that," Angela confirmed. "He created a space for Harvey, and then gave him all the support, encouragement, and praise that Harvey needed in order to succeed in that space.

It's kind of like taking care of a garden. You have to give the plants everything they need to grow strong and tall, right? A plant would not be able to survive without providing the right amount of water, sunlight, and air.

"It's the same thing with your employees. You need to provide the right kind of environment for them to grow and prosper. And, just as important, you have to continually support them by providing feedback on their performance, by checking in with them to make sure they feel like they are contributing. And they have to know that you will have their back!"

"Okay, I think I'm starting to get the hang of this now," Cynthia said. "But you said Otis said that he works for Harvey. Did you demote him or something?" Cynthia asked.

It was still inconceivable to her that some upstart like Otis could be bold enough to break the time-honored chains of command that the company had set in place ages ago.

Why would we even bother to have general managers and district managers and store managers if anyone could just assume leadership without the titles? she wondered.

Angela laughed out loud. "Otis says that the World's Lousiest Story is that our employees work for us." She studied the confused look on

Cynthia's face and tried yet again to get her to open her mind a bit more. Wouldn't you agree that you couldn't force someone to do something they don't *really* want to do?"

"Not really. I mean, I force my employees to do lots of things that they don't particularly want to do," Cynthia admitted. "I think that's what it means to be in a leadership position. If someone doesn't want to work, they can find another place to work! Certainly I did not become a district manager by disobeying direct orders from people above me! And now you're saying that my employees don't even work for me?"

"Tell you what," Angela began. "Let's go meet his team. I think you'll start to see what he means..."

The first thing Cynthia noticed about "the team" and the store was how busy it was. There was an odd feeling hanging over the establishment.

She could only describe it as pleasant, like the feeling you get when you walk into a beautiful garden filled with orchids and wildflowers and berries. She couldn't believe the feeling coming over her.

All of her pharmacies were located in much larger towns, and none of them were as busy as this small town location. Even as people waited patiently in long lines, she could not find one person who appeared to be disgruntled, upset, or angry.

Employees were zooming every which way and Otis resembled a conductor leading a symphony.

He was in the middle of the showroom, popping left to say hello to the people dropping off orders, then popping right to say hello to people picking up orders. Then he ended up in the middle answering questions from a few customers. There was no doubt he was the center of attention, but the way he went about it confused Cynthia.

He would ask customers about their children's ball games, the cast on their arms, and every form of small talk imaginable, but he never once talked about the pharmaceuticals he was selling.

Okay, this is really strange, Cynthia thought. *Is this a beauty parlor or a pharmacy?* All she could do was shake her head.

Angela grabbed Cynthia's left arm. "Okay, if we want to go meet the team, we're going to have to make a break for it. We could be standing here all day observing the activity before we even get a chance to say hello! Trust me, this store is always buzzing with excitement and activity."

Otis looked up and noticed the ladies entering the side door. He was already brimming with all the excitement in the world, but his eyes grew especially bright at the sight of Angela and Cynthia. Cynthia recoiled a bit; she was still a bit cautious about falling for the "Otis bug" and relinquishing her power to someone who she assumed to be working under her.

"Hey, guys, I want you to meet Cindy! "She's going to be joining our team in a few weeks." Otis announced to the rest of the group.

Some of the employees were still attending to customers, laughing and smiling with familiar strangers, but they took a few brief moments to wave and smile.

"Cindy, come on in and meet the stars of the organization!!" Otis said. Not missing a beat, he took over for some of the employees at the counter so they could meet Cynthia. He quickly zipped off to help a customer who had questions about vitamin supplements.

A friendly brunette name Missi was the first to approach Cynthia. "Glad to meet you Cindy! I have no doubt in my mind that you'll love being on our team!"

Cynthia was taken aback. Not only was this new person welcoming her to the team—again, of which she had assumed herself the leader—Missi had called her "Cindy," a name that no one had ever called her. "Well, um well, actually it is Cynthia. I'll just have to make sure that Otis knows that too."

"Oh, I'm sorry about that," Missi said. "But we're all friends here. If you don't want to be called Cindy, so be it!"

"Speaking of Otis, your boss is a piece of work, isn't he?" Cynthia stammered, taken aback by the way he introduced her, as if she was only the new cashier or something.

"Boss?" Missi replied. "Oh, I don't have a boss! He won't let us call him that. He says that *he works for us*, and that we are his bosses. But that's only the half of it. When it comes down to it, he's nothing but an overgrown six-year-old! He's such a goofball."

Cynthia remembered coming to that assessment after she witnessed all the Disney paraphernalia he was wearing. She raised her eyebrows as she began to question how he was able to become a pharmacy manager in the first place.

"I just love working with him!" Missi continued. 'Heck, I just plain love him!"

Cynthia nodded as she soaked in the words and enthusiasm Missi conveyed.

Then Cynthia turned to Angela and exclaimed with an exasperation-laden voice, "One of his employees just called him a goofball! Do you think he is really okay with that?"

"I don't know," Angela said smiling. "Why don't we ask him?" Angela was pretty sure she already knew the answer to that question, but she wanted to give Cynthia an opportunity to witness more of Otis's personality and lightness.

As Otis went by, Angela playfully grabbed his shoulder and said, in a teasing voice, "Hey Otis, Missi here just called you a goofball. Are you okay with that?"

Otis smiled, took two steps to the left, looked at Missi and put his right hand in the air as if to say "High Five!" and she high-fived him! Her respect for him was obvious to everyone in the room, but Cynthia.

As Otis turned back around, his face suddenly went stone cold serious. It was as if he were a cheetah and an antelope had entered his line of sight.

Without saying a word, he shot over to the prescription drop off window and displaced the person who was working there.

Before Cynthia knew what was happening, a very large and very angry man was lumbering up to the window and the first words out of his mouth were, "Am I going to have the same problems with you that I had with that f-ing racist across the street?"

Cynthia froze. Everyone else scattered. This man was at least six inches taller than Otis and easily outweighed him by fifty pounds. And he was really, really upset! Cynthia's curiosity grew; she wondered how the magnificent "O" was going to be able to turn this one around.

Otis was unbelievably calm and said jokingly, "Of course not! No one has problems with me... well, okay that's not true. My wife often has problems with me, but that's a whole other subject..."

The oversized man's expression turned from storming mad to slightly amused. But it was clear that he wasn't going to give up until he got the satisfaction he deserved. "What the heck happened across the street?" Otis continued.

"That blankety-blank racist at Hometown Pharmacy wouldn't fill my prescription! He said something about how the doctor didn't sign it, but I know he just didn't want to help me because he's a blankety-blank racist."

"Was he a bald guy about my height?" Otis asked, obviously trying to establish rapport with the customer.

"Yeah, that's the guy!" the big angry man stated with fire in his eyes. Otis shook his head in agreement.

"Oh, you mean Al!" Otis began. "Al's not a racist, sir. Al's a jerk to everybody. Why do you think we are so busy?" Otis quipped with a calm smile.

"Anyway, of course I can take care of this! All I have to do is call the doctor and confirm the prescription. I'll do that right away, and we'll have you back on the road in no time."

Then he excused himself so that he could go back to the office and make the call the to the doctor. He returned in a few minutes with a big smile on his face.

"Problem solved! Your doctor confirmed the prescription. He also apologized for providing you a prescription without including his signature."

"Oh," the man said. Suddenly, all the anger that the man was fuming was withering away. In its place was a firm smile of appreciation. "All right, well, thank you, sir."

"Please call me Otis."

"Okay, Otis," the man said, "I'm Pete. Thanks very much for getting this taken care of. I've been traveling on business and my lower back went out two days ago. I've been in severe pain since that time, and all I really needed was to get this prescription filled. At least now I can have a little time to heal before I move on to the next town!"

"Absolutely!" Otis cried. "Just let us know if there is anything else we can do for you while you're here in town. If I'm not here, any one of my other very capable and friendly workers can help you."

The man grabbed the bag with his prescription and gave Otis a firm handshake. "You really made my day, Otis. I just didn't know what I was going to do if I didn't get this medicine."

"No problem, Pete. Anytime!" Otis said, waving goodbye as Pete walked toward the store entrance.

Cynthia and Angela were wrapping up their study of the encounter with the previously angry man. "I think he handled that quite well, don't you think?" Angela asked Cynthia.

Cynthia nodded her head in agreement. She had to admit, when Otis used phrases like 'my other very capable and friendly workers,' it sounded like a sales pitch for a 1950's soap commercial.

But coming from Otis, it didn't feel awkward in the least. In fact, it sounded natural. And, as she continued to study the boundless energy of Otis, she was starting to have a change of heart about him.

Perhaps there was something to this guy, she thought to herself. Then she turned to Angela and answered her. "Yes, I think he handled that very well. The customer came in and he was obviously frustrated. He had a bad experience with another pharmacist and he brought that anger and negative energy into this store. But then, Otis was so tactful with this person that all of that negative energy had melted away before he left the store!"

"Yes!" Angela said. "Now think about this: what would have happened if Otis had ignored this man's bad mood? Do you think the customer would have walked out of here in a better mood?"

"I guess not," Cynthia surmised. "He probably would have remained ticked off."

"Right," Angela said. "And what do you think Otis did differently, such that he was able to turn a very obvious frown into a smile?"

While Cynthia thought about a response, she noticed that Otis was back to work. Without missing a beat, he bopped down to the other side of the showroom to help a woman pick out a cold medicine.

Cynthia couldn't help but wonder how he didn't have to take a break after such an alarming flare-up.

"I just don't know how to answer that question, Angela," Cynthia admitted. "I know what I would have done. I know that I would have tried to calm the customer down and I probably would have told him that we couldn't do anything about the guy across the street, but I would try to help him as best I could.

"So, to answer your question, it seemed like Otis didn't really care about how the customer was feeling—by that, I mean he didn't let the customer's mood affect his mood. And then he was able to get to the bottom of the issue and make the customer happy."

"That's just the tip of the iceberg," Angela said. She tapped Cynthia on the shoulder and said, "He loves it when things go wrong. It gives him a chance to shine."

"Hmm," Cynthia said. "So he likes chaos?" She thought to herself about how she did everything to avoid chaos in her life. But unfortunately, that wasn't working very well. Especially now that it was confirmed that she only had a measly thirty-two percent approval rating among her "team."

"Well, I think you've learned enough for one day, Cynthia," Angela said. "I've actually got to get some business stuff taken care of while I'm here." Angela went over to Otis, who had just wrapped up with the cold medicine lady.

"I need to go to the back to start inventory prep. Can you walk Cynthia out for me?"

"Sure thing," Otis said with a smile.

"Oh, by the way, I told her about the First Law!"

"Well, that's great!" Otis said. "It's always wonderful when other people can come to understand how things get done around here!" he added with a sly smile.

Cynthia was only slightly offended by his statement. She felt that she might have received all the training she thought she would need to lead her team.

"Come on, Cindy. Let's go find your car!" Cynthia wanted to correct his obvious mispronunciation of her name, but she was too busy trying to process all that had happened in the few moments she had been there.

As they were walking to the car Cynthia stopped, looked at Otis, and firmly stated, "You know what? I just don't get this whole boss-goofball thing!!"

Otis laughed a little and said knowingly, "Of course it doesn't make sense yet. We haven't talked about its importance!

"One of the corollaries of the Law of Contribution is that people will contribute to the degree that they feel important. By this definition, I am only important to the degree that I underscore the importance of others.

"The customers and the people that you think work for me need to feel supremely important if I am to create the best possible results. So my real job is to work as hard as possible to make *them* feel as important as possible. The company calls people and their work hours 'controllable expenses,' but I call them my greatest assets. It is really as simple as that."

As Cynthia approached her car, she remained as silent as possible. It was bad enough that she had received such bad news during her meeting with Rick. Add to that the worries she was facing on a daily basis just to make ends meet, support her family, and keep her job.

Finally, she was worried that she was being out shined by an upstart hotshot. It was all too much for her to digest in one day, but she kept moving confidently toward her car door.

Otis remained close by, again with a smile on his face, until she had successfully pulled out the parking lot.

Chapter Five

The Birthday Cake

On the drive home, she continued to think more about the day she had had. She thought maybe this Otis guy had a point, but his way of going about it seemed a little loony to her. Angela was clearly eating out of the palm of his hand, just like the employees who worked at the store.

She had so much swimming around in her head, so much that she would have to digest at some point, especially if she wanted to keep her job.

The last remaining question she had was about how Otis took care of the angry customer. Is it any wonder people loved coming into that store? *Heck, even I'd go to that store anytime I needed a pick-me- up!* she thought.

Eventually, she had to turn her attention to the task facing her at home, namely her son Tommy's birthday party. Tommy was turning five the following day and all of the relatives were coming over. As with any five- year-old, she knew that a birthday party was a big deal.

And, as his mother, she knew a lot of preparation would be underhand. It wasn't enough that this week had been very stressful and very long—she was in it on her own.

A couple days earlier, Don had gotten a callback for a job interview in another city. The interview was a few hours away, but if he got the job he would be able to mostly work from home.

It was an opportunity that Cynthia and Don agreed he couldn't afford to miss.

She wanted to just plop down on the couch as soon as she got home and sleep for the rest of the day. But that wasn't possible, at least not today.

Where her professional life ended, her family life began. And that life required her to make a big chocolate cake for Tommy, as well as all the other signs of festivity that came along with it.

Tommy gave her a big hug when she walked into the house and screamed, "Mommy!"

"Hi, big boy!" she said. "What have you been doing all day long? I see you got your crayons out. Did you draw me a picture?"

"Yes, Mommy," Tommy said with excitement. He waddled over to the dining room table, where he retrieved a white piece of paper from the table. "This is for you!" he shouted.

"Oh my, it's beautiful!" Cynthia said. "Thank you for making that for me!"

"You're welcome," Tommy said. Without wasting any more time, he started talking about what was really important to him. "Daddy called and said it's my birthday tomorrow. We are having a party!"

"Yes, that's right, Tommy," Cynthia agreed. "As a matter of fact, I'm going to start making that big chocolate cake for you, as soon as dinner is done."

"Yeah!" Tommy shouted. Then he started asking about all the friends and relatives who would be attending the party.

For a moment, Cynthia got caught up in her young son's enthusiasm and forgot about the drudgery of getting everything ready for the big day.

Immediately after dinner, she cleaned up the dishes and began to think about all of the things she needed to do to get ready for the party. *I'll be lucky if I get to bed before midnight,* she thought.

She was just on the verge of tears. Everything she had been through in the last few days was slowly starting to eat away at her confidence and resolve.

She didn't quite know how she was going to break the news about her performance to Don.

She had been putting off telling him about her evaluation because things had already been tense between them. They seemed to always fight over money. This week they disagreed over the expenses related to Tommy's party.

"He's just a five-year-old," Don had said to her, suggesting that the budget she proposed was a bit too high. "We've got other expenses right now, so we can't afford to spend a month's salary on our son's birthday party. He probably won't even remember it a week from now."

As she began to drag out the bowls and the measuring cups to make the cake, she felt a tug on her skirt. There was Tommy, anxious to help her make the cake for his special day.

"Can I help, Mommy?" he asked. The look in his bold brown eyes belied a sweetness that couldn't be ignored.

"Oh, Tommy," Cynthia said with a startled look on her face. "I thought you were watching television with Jared," she said in desperation.

As much as she wanted to let Tommy help with making the cake, she knew that it would take five times as long and be ten times as hard. And she was clearly in a position to save as much time as possible. Making the cake was just the beginning of the tasks she had set out to accomplish for the evening and any delay would affect the likelihood of her completing everything she needed to do.

"Jared is busy with school stuff," Tommy said in a cute five-year-old voice. She thought about calling to Jared to come get Tommy out of the kitchen so that she could just do it herself, but since he was upstairs doing his homework, getting him to watch Tommy while she attended to the kitchen duties wouldn't work either.

Monica wasn't home because of cheerleading practice. Cynthia felt really bad because she didn't want to upset her little birthday boy.

As she fished for any other options that she might have, she looked across the table at her bag. She saw the journal Angela had bought her.

"Honey, why don't you just sit at the dining room table for a minute, okay?" She reached into her bag and grabbed the journal.

"People need to feel important," Otis had said.

"Make sure everybody contributes," Angela had said.

Tommy was obviously not happy about having to sit at the table. In his five-year-old mind, he saw it as some type of punishment. It also said to him that Mommy didn't want him to help with the cake, which made him visibly upset. "Mommy, it's my cake!" Tommy suddenly called out.

"Oh, for the love of..." Cynthia forced out. She resigned herself to the state of affairs. Her young son was not going to let up and pretty soon he would be crying profusely.

"Okay, let's make your cake," she said. She grabbed his hand and led him back over to the other side of the kitchen. A flash of happiness landed on Tommy's face. A strange thing happened as they went to work.

Cynthia watched as Tommy's eyes beamed with pride because he was making his very own birthday cake. She also noticed that the project was not nearly as difficult as she had feared.

In fact, it was fun. It was just her and her little buddy making a cake. The time just flew by and they were both getting excited about how the cake was going to turn out.

They had carefully measured all of the ingredients and mixed them all together in a big bowl. Then, Tommy watched as his Mommy poured the batter into the glassware, grabbed the oven mitts and placed the cake into the oven.

When the cake was ready to come out of the oven, Tommy stood there wide-eyed with as much anticipation as he could muster. Finally, he shouted, "Yay!" as he soaked in the wonderful smells of freshly made cake.

When it came time to frost the cake, she gave him the bowl, the spatula, and told him to do his best. After much fussing about how to decorate it, she stepped back to witness a cake that looked like it had been made by a five year old.

She giggled a bit and patted Tommy on the head. "Good job, little guy!" she said.

For once in her life, Cynthia didn't care about the appearance of the cake. The only thing that mattered was the look on her son's face. It was clearly a Kodak moment, one that she had not seen in a very long time.

She paused for a moment when she realized that she had given her son the best possible present for his birthday: a chance to contribute.

On the day of the party, Tommy was dressed in his best outfit. He had handpicked it two days before and Cynthia made sure it was pressed and clean. As she helped Tommy get dressed for his big day, all he could talk about was how fun it was to make the cake with her.

That excitement continued to build as the relatives and friends started pouring in. Tommy greeted all of them with a booming, "Come see the cake I made!" and then his guests would "ooh" and "aah" at the marvelous site.

"You made this all by yourself?" his Aunt Jean asked.

"Well, Mommy helped, too. Mommy said the oven is too dangerous for me. She did that. But I put it all together. And I put the frosting on!"

The conversation happened many times that day and Tommy never tired of it. He was so very proud of himself. Cynthia was even prouder.

That evening as she was cleaning up, she noticed that the empty cake plate now looked exactly as it would have if she had made the cake by herself.

She began to wonder if the little things are indeed the big things. She definitely had a lot to think about.

She took out the journal Andrea had given her and under the words "The Law of the Contribution," she wrote a few notes:

"People need to feel important. I am only as important as I make others feel. People are assets and not expenses. Make sure everybody contributes and knows what their contributions are. Set them up to succeed. Then lavish them in authentic praise and reward them for the part they play in the team's victories."

Chapter Six

The Law of the Story

When Monday rolled around, she was a little nervous about going back to work. She had learned a few things from her young son about the importance of making other people feel important; it was evident to her that allowing Tommy to help make his birthday cake seemed to make all the difference in the world.

She even believed that it set the tone for the entire party, which was an overwhelming success! If only she could transfer some of that feeling of happiness to her job. But she was still not clear how she was going to do that.

As Cynthia thought about Otis, her employee satisfaction scores, and the many other problems she was currently facing, she couldn't get the image of her son out of her mind.

Not knowing what else to do, she went for a drive. She had no real plan when she started out, but eventually her car began to point itself north. She wanted so badly to believe that Otis could help her.

Angela said he could. But, seriously, what could he do? Surely the Law of the Contribution was starting to make more sense, but was there more to it than that?

Surely just giving people the space to feel important, to feel like they are contributing was one step on the path toward effective leadership.

But she just didn't get how she was supposed to turn to a guy who she would be evaluating in a professional capacity in just a few months.

Nevertheless, she ended up in the parking lot at Otis's store. She told herself she would go in and just talk to him. She just wanted to get to the bottom of this, even if it meant she had to bite her tongue a little bit.

Deep down she hoped he would do or say something that would show her that he was **not** the answer.

It just didn't make sense. How was someone in her position ever going to seek counsel from an underling?

She took her time strolling through the store. She busied herself with other things she would obviously be doing as a district manager: looking at shelves to make sure they were stocked, assuring that items had price tags on them, and assuring the overall cleanliness and presentation of the store.

As she made her way back to the pharmacy, she was half hoping it was Otis' day off. She needed to talk to him, but then she didn't really want to deal with his casual manner or his goofiness.

She was slightly shocked when she finally spotted Otis... talking to a... well she didn't know *what* it was. From behind, it was hard to discern if this guy had on a costume or was simply a "unique" individual.

When she got closer, it became even less clear.

Otis was waiting on a guy who was about six feet six inches tall with no hair. Well, that isn't exactly true. He did have "hair" in the sense of hair follicles that were actually a half-dozen ten-inch-long fluorescent green spikes, located where a mohawk would normally be.

The man had a black leather jacket over his shoulder, and he was wearing black leather pants. The muscle shirt he was wearing showed off his incredibly muscular arms, which were strewn with intricately detailed, colored snake tattoos that appeared to be biting the head off of a cat.

She noticed he had a brass chain that connected his gold nose ring to his earring that resembled a shark. He was really quite a sight.

Cynthia surmised that he was probably some sort of biker... or maybe he was a bouncer at a nightclub. Maybe he was in a gang.

Whoever he was, it was clear that he was not to be messed with, unless you wanted a trip to the hospital. Standing upright, he didn't move much as he seemed to be paying close attention to Otis.

Otis was speaking to him as if he was giving him an intense set of directions. The biker dude didn't move a muscle. It was as if he was a statue.

All of a sudden, both men burst out in uproarious laughter. Their laughter continued as Otis reached below the counter. He came up and handed the biker dude his prescription and a tissue.

"Here, Steve," Otis said in a jovial tone. "Wipe away those tears of laughter. Oh, make sure you take this with plenty of water, and make sure that you don't take it on an empty stomach. I really don't want to have to find something else for you if you come in here and grumble about how badly your tummy hurts!"

"Okay, Mommy!" Steve laughed.

Mommy? Cynthia thought. Of all the names she had imagined people calling Otis, Mom was not one of them. But, as she further inspected the situation, she believed that Steve was receiving advice that could be seen as motherly.

She watched as Otis laughed it off and went on with his conversation. He didn't get upset by the name and he continued, just like he did with the angry out-of-towner.

"All right, get outta here," Otis replied playfully.

When Steve left and Otis turned around, one of his newest cashiers, a woman named Joan, was standing there scowling at him.

Otis looked at her, and Joan said very sternly, "I cannot believe you are so nice to Mohawk Guy! He looks creepy. And he's a bit of a freak. Who walks around with spikes on top of their head? Not anyone I know."

Otis smiled and said: "Who, Steve? It's just your first week, Joannie. You'll soon realize I'm not allowed to make value judgments about other people... ever."

That set her back a step and she had to ask what he meant about not being allowed—which was, of course, what he was going for.

Cynthia was taken aback as much as the new cashier and eagerly awaited Otis's response.

Otis continued, "Joanie, do you realize a few years ago I was suffering from horrible job stress, and I had to go on medicine for anxiety and high blood pressure?"

"Really?" she said. "I can't imagine someone like you being stressed out."

He nodded and continued, "I was scared I had lost myself as well. I really didn't know what I could do to get myself back together again. But I knew something had to be done. So I started doing my research.

"I looked at myself like a science project. What causes stress? What happens in our brain that so afflicts the body? I took a deep look into the brain and the psychology of stress. After several months of research, both online and offline, I uncovered the craziest psychological diagnosis you'll ever hear."

"And what is that?" Joan asked. "ANTs were eating my brain!" Otis calmly stated.

"Okay," Joan said with a slight pause, "so you're telling me that you had ants living inside your head... and that they were eating your brain? I'm no doctor, but I am sure if that was true, I would have heard of that."

Otis laughed and made a mocking gesture where he held his head toward the counter and used the base of his palm to tap the side of his head, as if he was studying the counter to see if any ants were forced out.

"ANTS stands for Automatic Negative ThoughtS. During my research I came upon the work of Dr. Daniel Amen. I learned that as we go through our day, we have roughly 60,000 random thoughts. The more we allow those thoughts to be negative, disempowering, and judgmental, the more ANTs eat our brain alive.

"When I learned that people with unresolved anxiety and depression issues have as much as a fifty percent greater incidence of Alzheimer's Disease, I immediately put myself on a five-step regimen to banish ANTS from my brain forever."

Oh no, Cynthia thought. *Here comes another one of his homemade remedies.* She shook her head in amazement as she pondered the depth of his imagination.

It was a wonder to her that a man like Otis could survive in the world she lived in.

Regardless, she continued to listen in on the conversation. Perhaps there was something in it for her.

After Joan had sat there for a few moments, desperately trying to process what Otis had said, Otis got to the crux of her curiosity.

"So would you like to know what those five steps are?" he asked her politely. She sort of just nodded in disbelief. The Alzheimer's statistic seemed to have entranced her. "Well, here they are!"

1) "I refuse to 'value judge.' Value judging is nothing more than a bad habit. When we value judge others, our brain sees it as something we always do. So, it causes us to also value judge ourselves. And you probably already know that we are our own worst critics."

2) "I write in a thought journal. Negative thoughts about our situation, our environment and ourselves become so engrained over time that they actually turn into impulses and feelings. Negative impulses and feelings are scary because they seem so real. If left unchecked, they actually become real. So, to break the cycle, I wrote down my negative thoughts, feelings, and impulses. Then, I challenged their validity. I actually argue *against* them, and not *for* them, as I did when I was losing myself."

3) "I keep a fat rubber band on my wrist and snap it whenever I catch myself going down a negative path. This 'snaps' me back to reality and creates a small punishment—sometimes I snap it very hard— for poor-quality thinking."

4) "I feed my brain positive information in the form of quotes, sayings, music, images and friends every single day to teach my brain how much I care about it and about keeping it healthy."

5) "I adopt an 'or you can think...' mentality. Whenever a negative thought enters my head, I change it to a positive one. In the case of Steve it would go like this: If I thought of him as a creepy Mohawk guy, I would say to myself, '...or you could think about how awesome it is that he creatively expresses himself without hurting anybody else. I admire his courage.'"

He went on to explain to Joan, "Thoughts are just things. Although they seem real, they are not. Everyone thinks things that no one else should ever hear."

That is completely normal. But when you give yourself an opportunity to challenge your own thought process, the better chance you have of making good choices.

"If I went around thinking that anyone who looked different from me or talked with a heavier accent than me was somehow not worthy of my respect, I would never be able to serve people. But, the more I challenge my thoughts, the more they tend to improve. As they improve, everything in my life improves right along with them."

"So I can change the way I see other people by simply challenging my own thoughts?" Joan asked, obviously more curious than she had been earlier.

"Yes! Consider the alternatives. Is it hard work? Yes! In fact, it's excruciating to have to always monitor what I am thinking so that it doesn't become a standard way of behaving! But, Alzheimer's Disease is no picnic either!"

"Wow," Joan finally said, "you certainly have a point there. So, the longer I hold onto negative thoughts, and the more they become standard ways of dealing with situations in life, the more likely I am to have some type of disease when I get older?"

"It could be any number of things, Joanie," he replied. "People suffer from all sorts of illnesses as a result of the negative thoughts they have held onto for a long time. Some people start to believe the negative thoughts about themselves and it leads to crippling depression. Some people might try to deal with those thoughts by drinking or taking drugs, and then have to suffer through health complications that are very costly. And, in the case of Mohawk Steve, I might end up in the hospital for making some snide remark that sets him off.

"So the only thing I can do is control how I approach things. If I make a value judgment about someone, now, with this new way of approaching things, I can challenge it with one of my 'or you could think...' statements, and it totally turns the whole conversation around!"

"Wow, okay," Joan said, with a little shock in her voice. She apologized for the value judgment she had made about Steve, and then scurried off to grab a pen. It appeared as though she wanted to write down some of the things Otis had said about ANTs.

Cynthia was also taken aback. Being able to control negative thoughts was something she had never even considered before.

Is that really possible? she thought. *Have I truly lost control over my thoughts?* She thought about all things she had been thinking just about Otis since she first heard Angela's glowing praise of him.

At first, she thought he was some sort of superstar. And then, upon seeing him in the flesh, she had surmised that he was just a goofy kid who floated through life without a care in the world.

Hearing him admit that he had a problem with his thoughts and then sought to deal with it certainly made her feel more optimistic about her own situation.

She was determined to get rid of her own ANTS now. When Otis realized Cynthia was standing there, he greeted her warmly. "Oh, Cindy! Welcome to the ANT farm!" he said, and then smiled warmly.

"Oh," she said, not knowing exactly how to respond. She didn't want him to think she was spying on him, but she was also very curious to know how to get rid of her own ANTS.

So she took it upon herself to inquire further about the negative thoughts. At this point, she was ready to do just about anything to help her battle the demons of guilt and self-doubt.

"Well, I overheard a bit about what you were saying to..." she began, not remembering the girl's name.

"Joanie," he said. "Joanie, I'd like you to meet Cindy. She's going to be a part of our team very soon." Joan held out her hand to shake Cynthia's.

"And do you have questions about what I was saying?" Otis asked.

"Yes, I do," Cynthia said. "How to do you get rid of negative thoughts that keep recurring? The kind that seems to cripple you to such an extent that they never go away?"

"Well, first of all," Otis began, "you're never really helpless when it comes to thoughts. It's just a matter of getting underneath them and stopping the cycle from becoming a bad habit. It's really about what I call the Law of the Story. Our lives are only as good as the stories that we tell ourselves. Want a better life? Then you have to tell yourself a better story!"

"You mean like how you said Steve was creatively expressing himself without hurting anybody else?" Cynthia chimed in. She was starting to feel a little more confident with the whole idea.

"So you were spying on us!" Otis said. Cynthia's eyes grew wide, and she started to think about how it would look to her employees to know that she was spying on them.

"I was just kidding," Otis finally said. Joan and Cynthia both laughed, although Cynthia's laugh was more of the nervous kind. "That's one aspect for sure," Otis confirmed, "but the most important aspect is in the stories we tell ourselves about ourselves!"

When we need to make a change in our lives, we have to tell ourselves a story about how we can make that change happen.

"Okay," Cynthia said.

"It is all too easy to tell yourself why you can't make a change! Do you know what I mean?"

Cynthia knew what he meant. "You mean like when we say that we don't have enough time or money or smarts to do something we really want to do, right?"

"Exactly!" Otis was happy to see she got the point. "You definitely have 'the smarts,' Cindy! You are very bright, you know!"

"If only," she said meekly.

Before she dropped the big bombshell that was her life, she looked at both Otis and Joan cautiously.

Finally, believing that she was in good company, she started to spill the beans. "I am really struggling at my job and my employee approval rating is super low. I really don't know how to turn that around. I know that if I get another bad evaluation from Rick, I won't have a job for much longer.

"And, when I think about that, about not being able to support my family, it makes my stomach ache. So it just continues like that over and over. I keep thinking that maybe I'll have a better go at things when I get up every morning, but then something happens and I fall back into my less-than-stellar self. It ends up affecting everything that I touch, including my employees."

"I see," Otis said. Suspecting that Cynthia really needed some one-on-one time, he asked Joan to check the floor for any customers who might need help selecting a product. Joan dismissed herself and uttered an amicable "nice to meet you" to Cynthia.

"I was kind of hoping you could help me with all of this," Cynthia said. "In fact, Angela suggested that I come talk to you."

"Of course I'll help you!" Otis said, hoping to make her feel better. He knew how tough it must have been for her to come to him for help.

"I'll tell you what, Thursday I have to be at the car dealership near your office for recall repair. It should only take like twenty or thirty minutes. I have a ton of fun things I want to do for the rest of the morning, but I can meet you for lunch around noon. Does that work?"

Cynthia nodded in agreement. She was relieved to not have to drive another four hours round trip to chat with Otis and also that he was so kind about it.

Tuning into her feelings, she immediately noticed that she was a bit lighter and happier than she was when she had first walked into the store.

"Friday, I have to meet Allen, the pharmacy manager at your Altoona store. He asked me for advice on 'how to get his people to work harder' and it might be good for you to hear what I have to say.

"I subbed at his store during his vacation, and he wants to know what I thought. I don't think he's going to like my report. Do you want to meet with us?"

"That would be great," Cynthia said. "We have had all kinds of personnel issues in that store, and any help you can offer would be really appreciated. We've been considering making some personnel changes there. Maybe you can provide us with some insights on a course of action." Cynthia blurted out, cautiously excited about this Mickey Mouse fan club guru potentially being able support her decision to replace a few people.

"That store needs a change in philosophy, not personnel," Otis said, slightly off the cuff. "Don't worry; I'll tell you everything I have seen in that store, and I promise you that I won't let my ANTS speak for me!

"But, let's save that for Friday. Now, if you'll excuse me..." Otis said, motioning with his eyes to some approaching customers.

"All right, I'll let you get back to it then," Cynthia said.

"In the meantime, start thinking about how you can change the story you tell yourself. When you are faced with a situation that is difficult, say, Allen's store, try coming up with some 'or you could think...' statements.

See if that doesn't change the way you approach things!"

As she turned around to leave the store, she took one last glance at Otis. By then he had busied himself with the new customer, flashing his broad smile and the gentle nature he was possessing.

She thought that maybe he had come up with some value judgment about the customer—maybe about the hat she was wearing—but she also knew that somehow, someway, he was able to look past those thoughts and really serve the customer.

It was something that still baffled her, but she knew that all the answers would come very soon. She wasn't sure how Otis would help her, but she tried to tell herself a story that was cautiously optimistic.

Chapter Seven

A Better Story

By the time Cynthia had arrived at home it was after eight p.m. Her spur-of-the-moment road trip had put her behind; she spent the rest of the day in her office trying to catch up. She was grateful for the opportunity to spend some time at Otis' store.

She found herself started to warm up to his style, and his ideas were slowly infiltrating her thoughts.

She was concentrating on the "better story" that Otis was talking about. *How would I go about creating a better story?* she thought as she gazed at the journal Angela had given her.

She closed her eyes for a moment, and then took in a long breath and exhaled slowly.

An image of her childhood came into view. She was about ten years old at the time, and her family was going on a road trip to Yellowstone National Park.

They had been traveling around the region for ten days, visiting natural landmarks to the north and east. When they finally made to a camping area near their final destination, they were showing signs of fatigue.

Cynthia's father was never known for being able to handle his emotions well. And when something went wrong, he very often took it out on Cynthia's mother and her two brothers.

Cynthia was especially sensitive, so whenever her father laid into her, she was especially hurt.

As the family was packing up to make the half-day journey to Yellowstone, Cynthia's father noticed that the car wouldn't start. He had tried several times for it to turn over, but to no avail. He popped the hood and inspected all the components to make sure that everything was in order.

He later discovered that he needed a new spark plug, which would have been fine had they been closer to civilization. But they were at least sixty miles from the nearest town, and there was nothing around except pine trees, red rocks and wildlife.

That discovery made Cynthia's dad flip his lid.

"Goddamnit!" Cynthia's father yelled, his bold voice echoing through the canyon walls. "I can't believe this! I should have bought a few parts for this damned trip. Why didn't I just get them?"

Cynthia's mother, who tended to be rather quiet and agreeable, tried everything she could to calm her husband down. But he was just too worked up to even take the cue.

In an effort to shield the kids from that volcano that was soon to erupt with fire and ash, she encouraged Cynthia and her brothers to head down to the river and spend some time enjoying nature.

The temperatures were quite mild and pleasant, and they would have a great time exploring.

"Chris," she said to the eldest sibling, "you look after your brother and sister. Don't go very far, and make sure you keep an eye on them."

Chris agreed, and then shuttled his two siblings with him down a hiking trail that led to the river's edge.

An hour later, the kids returned to the campground and noticed that their mother was sitting at a picnic table reading a book. She smiled widely as her three treasures came into view. "What did you find?" she asked with enthusiasm.

Chris piped up with excitement, "We found a turtle, and we were trying to catch some of the fish in the river," he said. "We didn't get anything worth saving, so we just threw 'em back."

"Good for you!" their mother said. Then she looked over at the car, still sitting there with its hood agape. "Your father hitched a ride to town so that he could get the parts he needs for the car. He should be back pretty soon.

"Why don't you guys sit here, and I'll get something ready for lunch." The kids formed a single-file line and headed toward the picnic table, eager for a bit of food to nourish their stomachs.

When their father returned to the campsite, he had a very relieved look on his face. Cynthia's mother thought that the anger had blown over and that everything would be right as rain once again.

The kids were finishing up their lunch and were eager to start playing again. Chris pulled Cynthia's pigtails, which forced her to retaliate. Chris ran into the woods, trying to escape, and Cynthia followed behind. They were all laughing and giggling and screaming at the tops of their lungs.

While Cynthia's mother found the fun in what they were doing, her father was not pleased. He had gone to town to get the parts he needed, but he was still frustrated that something like this had happened while they were a hundred miles away from home.

When Cynthia and Chris rounded their way back to the campsite, things took a very drastic turn.

"What the heck are you guys doing right now?" he asked in a very bold tone. "Can't you see that I really need to concentrate on what I'm doing? Or would you rather just sit and rot here for the rest of your lives?"

Cynthia and Chris instantly froze upon hearing their father's booming voice. They looked down at the pine needles on the ground, and they didn't look up. Cynthia thought that by giving her father some context about the situation he would have a change of heart.

"But, Daddy, Chris was being mean to me. He grabbed my hair and pulled it!"

"I really don't care what happened," her father uttered. "I don't want to hear another word. Cynthia, you should know better. Your mother and I taught you better than that. Sometimes I think we've failed as parents, because you act like you have no home training whatsoever."

"But, Daddy, I—"

"Enough!" he shouted, his voice again echoing throughout the rock canyon. "You don't listen very well, do you? You really need to learn some respect. When I say, 'I don't want to hear another word,' I mean it! Now shut your trap, or I'm going to leave you here for the bears and mountain lions."

Cynthia burst into tears shortly thereafter. Her sobbing trailed off as she ran with all her might back down the trail.

She just wanted to get as far away as she could and be alone to drown in her sorrows. Chris had attempted to follow her, but his father told him to stay put and help him with fixing the car.

Cynthia sat at her desk thinking about how hurt she had felt that day. She remembered how she sat at the water's edge and listened the soothing sounds of the river as it smashed into rocks and weaved its way toward the valley below. Her tears continued for ten minutes and she buried her head between her knees.

She thought that her father was serious about leaving her in the woods, and the thought of that, even as an adult, had continued to haunt her. *Why would Daddy have said that to me?* she wondered. *Did he not love me? Was I incapable of being loved like my brothers?*

But then she snapped back to the reality of her life in the present day. She thought about what Otis had said. And then she said something very earth shattering: "Or I could think..."

When she arrived home and walked in the house it was eerily quiet. She sensed that the kids were upstairs in their rooms, and hoped they were asleep.

When she walked into their home office she was startled by her husband Don. He was sitting at his desk with his hands over his face. "Honey, what's wrong?" she asked, but Don didn't say anything. He just looked up at her with his innocent puppy dog eyes and then shook his head.

She could tell that he had been crying, which scared her half to death, because Don never cried. They had been married for fifteen years, and she could not remember a period in all that time when he had broken down.

She rushed over to him. "What in God's name is wrong?" she asked in a panic-stricken voice.

After an excruciatingly long pause, Don blurted out: "I just can't do it! I just can't! I'm too old to keep up with all those young brilliant kids!! I just can't do it!"

She was so relieved she almost laughed. But, she didn't dare. She knew that he was referring to the "kids" in his classes, who were half his age. Don had lots of worries about going back to school. When his back and knees started showing signs of damage from years of working construction, he saw it as an opportunity to move into a new stage of life, one that Cynthia was very supportive of.

Still, this did not allay his fears about being in the classroom, about performing at optimum levels, and graduating with a degree in information technology. He wanted to be able to support his family, and being out of the workforce was starting to take its toll on him.

Interestingly enough, he had done pretty well in his first two years of classes. But because they had moved, he had now ended up at a higher ranked school, and the competition was very steep.

Cynthia loved him with every fiber of her being, but the truth was that ever since they relocated, they weren't getting along very well.

She blamed her job stress. He blamed his tough academic struggles. They had simply refused to work together, and it was wearing on both of them.

She really didn't know what to do or say, so she walked out of the room and began nervously putting her things away. Then she froze in her tracks.

Her thoughts had taken her back to her office, to the vision of her younger self and her final thought before she headed home. A smile flashed across her face.

She walked back into the home office and said loudly and firmly, "What a lousy story!"

Don's head popped up in disbelief, and his eyes opened extremely wide as if to say, "What?"

Cynthia said slowly and carefully, "The Donny I know is the man that worked fourteen hours a day building houses so that I could go to Management School. The Donny that is my knight in shining armor pounded nails until his hands bled so his children could eat.

"The Donny I know had to do all he could to get out of bed most days because his back and knees were so sore he could barely straighten up, and yet he went to work anyway, because his customers counted on him."

"This Donny that I'm seeing now needs to talk to *that* Donny and learn to tell himself a better story about what he can and cannot do!" Cynthia said with kind of a growl in her voice. She was quite satisfied with what she had told her husband, even though Don was shocked at her outburst. But, although she could tell that it had planted a seed in his mind, he was rendered speechless.

Not knowing what to do or say next, Cynthia quickly scurried out of the room, went upstairs, and got ready for bed.

She hoped Don would come upstairs and tell her she wasn't too hard on him or at least tell her something that would affirm his belief in what she had said. But he didn't. He was just quiet and unresponsive.

She was scared that she had messed up, and she soon fell asleep, drifting away from all the thoughts and conversations and frustrations of the day.

When she woke up, she noticed that Don was not sleeping beside her.

She began to panic. *Oh no; what have I done?* she thought. *Have I pushed him too far? Have I totally wrecked my marriage?*

He had never not come to bed before. As she picked up her bathrobe a card fell off of it. She picked it up and read the envelope, which read, "To my perfect angel!" It was clearly written in Don's handwriting.

She was stunned. It had been so long since he had called her that. She truly couldn't remember the last time he had gotten her a card for no real reason. When she opened the card, there was a picture of a computer-generated angel on the inside, probably the most beautiful angel she had ever seen!

The inscription read: "How do you like the logo I created last night? I created it just for you, my perfect angel, who said exactly the right thing at exactly the right time."

Now it was her turn to cry. When she went downstairs there was another note on the kitchen table: "Went to the library. Those young kids are going to have to get up awfully early if they are going to keep up with me!! Love, D."

Cynthia laughed and let loose another tear of joy. She pulled out her new journal and wrote on the second page:

"Law Number Two: The Law of the Story

If you want your life to get better, you have to tell yourself a better story!

Any story that begins with "I can't" is a lousy story.

Lousy stories give you ANTS! Yuck!"

Chapter Eight

The Law of the Agenda

As Thursday morning rolled around, Cynthia found herself strangely on edge, but she also had a little curiosity on her mind.

Thinking about how such a simple thing as changing the story she told herself, she realized that things were starting to look better for her.

What she had said to her husband, a direct result of the ongoing relationship Cynthia had with Angela and Otis, had completely revolutionized the way her husband saw his life.

For the last few days, he had been spending more hours in the library, and he was also paying more attention to her and the kids when he was at home! *What's not to love about that?* she thought.

If Otis could continue to feed her good ideas that would affect her personal life, surely it would also extend to her professional life. Perhaps then would she start to live a happier life.

At eight-thirty a.m., she checked her watch, thinking that maybe she could catch him while he was at the dealership and sidestep the whole lunch thing.

She wasn't averse to the idea of sitting down to lunch with him, but she found herself growing eager for the one-on-one contact she was scheduled to have hours later.

But then she remembered that Otis was planning to do some "fun stuff" in the morning before their lunch meeting. So she tried to keep herself occupied for a few hours until the scheduled meeting time. A few times she even opened up her journal and look at her handwritten contents.

She was beginning to see that the more she concentrated on the "laws" she had been given, the more everything was starting to sink in.

Otis decided to call her at eleven thirty. "Hi, Cindy. How are you?" he asked.

"I'm doing okay, Otis. How are you?"

"Well, I'm still at the dealership. Apparently, they ran into some problems. They keep apologizing and telling me that it will be done soon, but it's almost noon now, and I'm not sure what is going on."

"Oh, okay," Cynthia replied. She was a bit upset by the news, thinking that it was time to blame the auto mechanics for screwing up her very important lunch meeting.

"Well, if we need to reschedule our appointment, I can understand. There's not really much you can do if you car is being ripped apart."

"What do you think about meeting me here? We could just go over to the café across the street. Unless you were set on going to that fancier restaurant downtown..."

"Oh, no," Cynthia said. "That's fine." Then she started to giggle.

"Why are you laughing?" Otis asked.

"Well, I was just thinking about something—very much in line with your way of handling things."

"Oh," Otis said with a hint of curiosity.

"Yeah. I was thinking about how the auto mechanics had messed up our lunch meeting. I was thinking about how they were nothing but a bunch of liars who overcharge for the simplest little thing, and they always keep you there in their cold, unforgiving shop longer than you'd really like to be there.

"But then I told myself a different story!"

"Yeah?" Otis said.

"That's right!" Cynthia continued. "I thought that the fact that your car was still at the mechanics would give us a new opportunity that wasn't available before. We'll have the opportunity to try out a new café, for one..."

"That's a good way to see it," Otis said. "And I'm sure there are many other wonderful things that can come out of this that we couldn't have seen a few days ago."

"Well, I, for one, am ready to see what this meeting has in store for me. So, yes, I'll go ahead and meet you at the dealership, and we can take it from there!"

She pulled up to the dealership shortly before noon. When she walked inside, she saw Otis at the service counter with a very frantic looking young man who appeared to be checking him out. As she walked closer she could make out the name on his uniform, which was Frank, and she surmised that he was the service manager. The exchange she witnessed between the two men completely amazed her:

Frank began nervously. "Well, Otis, I just want to emphasize that it's not very often that we have things fall apart the way they did this morning.

"I really appreciate your patience with us. In fact, I cannot believe how patient you were. You must not have much going on today."

Otis replied calmly and cheerfully: "As a matter of fact, I had a lot of things planned today. Today is my fun day, and I was planning to do lots of fun stuff. But being here a bit longer doesn't bother me, nor does it mean I still can't do lots of fun stuff! Today will just be another kind of fun day. I'm excited about what the rest of the day has in store for me!"

Frank appeared to be amazed. "Wow! Thank you for being so patient! I can't tell you how many times I've had to break the news to someone who was sitting anxiously in the waiting room. Most of the time it doesn't go as well as this."

Otis said, as he turned to walk away, "No problem. Oddly enough it has more to do with acceptance than patience. You have a great day."

Frank seemed surprised by Otis's comment. "Wait!" he said excitedly. "I know you've been here forever already, but could you help me understand something?"

"Uh, sure," Otis said.

"I mean, I would have blown my top if I was you. I'm always blowing my top when 'things don't go right.' I mean, look at me. I'm a mechanic at a very busy auto dealership, and I know that sometimes customers have to wait a bit longer for their cars.

"But the way you are acting, it's like you had planned to stay here all day! Now, I know that's not the case, because you just told me about your plans today.

"So, I guess my question is this: how do you keep yourself from blowing up—at me or anyone else here—about the fact that you're still here? I'm always blowing up about stuff like this. Especially at home! And then I end up hating myself!"

Otis turned around, walked back to the counter, and kindly said, "Sure, I used to be like that in some ways, and it was killing me, too! Literally. Stress and anxiety had taken over my life, and I had to learn about ANTs, monkeys, agendas, and attachment."

Frank was hanging on his every word. "How do you mean?"

"Well, take today," Otis said. "I could tell myself a story about how the auto shop messed up my agenda by keeping me here. Right?"

"Right," Frank said. "That's what I would have thought."

"But, what a lousy story that would be! I'd have to carry that sucker around for the whole day, or maybe even several days. Instead, through writing, studying, coaching, and more studying, I have learned that the universe had a different agenda for me today.

"So, I had a *choice*, I could continue to be in conflict with an agenda I cannot change, or I could change my agenda to complement what the universe has in store for me today. So, you actually did me a favor. You gave me a quiet and uninterrupted space to read 175 pages of an amazing book called *Pushing to the Front* by Orison Swett Marden. So, I am really indebted to you, and I thank you!"

Frank was entranced. "Seriously?"

Otis went on. "Sure. If you stop and think about it, all relationships work that way. Today I need to, if I want to be happy, add value to my relationship with the universe by altering my agenda. When I get home I may have to alter my agenda to add value to my relationships with my wife and my son. It really is no different from that.

"The point is that when I am willing to alter my agenda, I am not sacrificing it. I am changing it to flow with and not against the current situation. The stress starts to come in when there is resistance to an agenda I cannot change. Just like I cannot change the agenda of the universe, I cannot change the agenda of another person. I can only reject someone else's agenda, or work within it. Rejection costs a lot in terms of emotional currency."

Frank countered with a defeated tone of voice. "But you don't understand! I cannot control my emotions like that!"

"Actually, I understand completely," Otis said with confidence.

"You've made an agreement with the monkeys that live on your back that you will keep feeding them, and that they will hang around forever. You might want to rethink that agreement."

"Monkeys?" Frank asked. Then he took the opportunity to look at his shoulders to make sure there were no monkeys hanging around. Otis laughed a bit before continuing.

"After years of study and research, I made a fun but very serious website to help people who are attached to the lousy stories that ruin their lives.

"You can check it out at *www.thesuccessfulthinker.com*. I think it would really help you find some of the answers you are looking for, and my contact information is all over it if you have questions."

Frank just shook his head in amazement. "Wow," was all he could say. And then he enthusiastically asked, "Anything else?"

Otis continued as if conversations like this were an everyday occurrence for him. "Just one thing. You are a nice man and you deserve an awesome life. I bet it would help you to spend a little time meditating on a simple yet critical question: 'What has losing my cool cost me?' Once you do that, with a little practice you'll stop feeding those monkeys, and you'll thank yourself for doing it!"

"Amazing!" Frank shouted. "Okay, I'm going to check out that website when I get home. Thank you very much for impacting my day in such a positive way!"

"You're very welcome," Otis said.

"Have a magical day," he continued, "I'm gonna go figure out what is next on the universe's agenda!"

As Otis turned around once again and began to move towards the door, he noticed Cynthia standing at the entrance. Cynthia, having spied on him yet again, was obviously cheerful and bright.

He smiled and said, "Hey, Cindy! Thanks so much for meeting me here today. Let's go see what the universe is going to feed us! I'm starving! By the way, how are you?"

"I'm doing okay," Cynthia said. At the same time she had some thoughts that she didn't want to convey to Otis. *Why does he insist on calling me Cindy? My name is Cynthia!* But those thoughts were quickly erased as she tried to play back in her mind what had just happened.

Otis had spent, by her math, something like three extra hours at the dealership... and he actually had made Frank, the service manager, feel good about it! *Did he really just thank the guy for the opportunity the wait time afforded him to read a book?*

Otis noticed the expression on Cynthia's face, which spoke to the utter confusion resting just behind her eyes.

"You sure you're okay?" Otis asked.

"Oh, I'm fine," she said. "Yes, let's go to lunch." Her original anxieties had been displaced by a strange curiosity to learn more about this whole "agendas" thing.

As Cynthia and Otis headed over to the café, Cynthia noticed a spring in Otis' step. In fact, he seemed to be almost walking on air.

Later, after they had been seated by a young college aged waitress, Cynthia noticed as Otis playfully conversed with the young lady.

She didn't appear to be in a very festive mood when she seated them, but after talking to Otis for a few moments, she was walking on sunshine.

After they ordered, Cynthia couldn't hold it in her curiosity any longer. She blurted out, "I don't get it! How are you so happy? Your plans got totally derailed! And you had all of these fun things planned for the day. Not that I know what that means, but anyway. Doesn't any of this bother you even a little?"

Otis looked at Cynthia and smiled. He seemed to be amused by her question.

"I would have been a few years ago," he said quietly. "But now I understand The Law of the Agenda!"

"There's that word again! Agenda!" Cynthia said wanting to get her mind around the concept. She remembered hearing Otis talk about agendas. Something about him having an agenda and how that agenda got disrupted somehow, and now he's on some other agenda. But how it all came together was still a bit of unclear.

"All stress is caused by conflicting agendas. For instance, many people make it a habit to steamroll someone else's agenda so that they can push their own agendas," Otis started to say.

"Steamrolling?" Cynthia asked quietly not sure of the term. "I'm not sure I understand what you mean by that."

"Well," Otis began, "picture a steamroller in your mind."

"Okay," she said as she pictured a huge hunk of machinery with a big, heavy roller where the front wheels would normally be. She pictured it heading down a closed section of highway. "All right. I'm seeing a steamroller."

"Good! Now, what's happening to the asphalt below the roller?"

"Well... it's getting flattened, right?" she said, hoping that she had answered the question correctly.

"Exactly. So think of the asphalt as your plans. Then think about the steamroller as someone else who just comes in and flattens your nice asphalt."

"Ah," she said with satisfaction.

"Now let's look at it with a different scenario that you might be familiar with. Has your boss ever called and said something to the effect that you should drop what you are doing and work on HIS problem?"

"Of course," she said, thinking that was sort of a no-brainer. "All managers do that, don't they?" Cynthia asked meekly, knowing full well she specialized in doing that to her own employees.

"The good ones don't," Otis said calmly correcting her. "Successful leaders are successful thinkers. They find out what the other person's concerns and agendas are, and then do their best to merge their direction to complement the other person's agenda.

"This allows the employee to feel 'heard' and feel 'valued.' Steam-rolled employees will, at best, give you forced compliance. But valued employees give you willing cooperation. There is a powerful difference between the two."

Cynthia was spellbound and just kind of stared at Otis. Looking at her own management style, she felt that forcing everyone to do things was the only way things actually got done. *My employees would just sit around and slouch on the counters were it not for my no-nonsense... steamrolling.*

"All relationships work that way." Otis continued. "If husbands and wives have competing agendas, their relationship becomes pretty dysfunctional or dissolve completely. But, if they can forge identical or at least complementary agendas, they become an unstoppable couple!

"Always remember, there's a reason water doesn't flow uphill!"

Chapter Nine

A Teenage Drama Queen

As Cynthia and Otis walked back to the car dealership to pick up their vehicles, she marveled at the way he was still bouncing and at his ability to be totally "tuned in" to those around him.

Not only had he made instant friends with the young waitress, he found time to make small talk with the bus boy, and several customers of the restaurant. He even ran into a woman who was a regular patron at his pharmacy who was also in town on business. It was a wonder that Otis had found any time to eat his own lunch since he seemed so busy "entertaining".

"Tell you what," Otis said, still bouncing around with all the enthusiasm he could muster, "I'd love to spend the rest of the day with you but, as you can already guess..."

"You have lots of fun things planned for the afternoon?" Cynthia added.

"Exactly," Otis said.

As he headed over to his car, he turned and waved. "See you tomorrow?"

"Will do," she said. Then, taking cues from Otis's boundless energy, she said, "Enjoy the rest of your day!"

Cynthia knew what the universe's agenda held in store for her, at least for the rest of the day. She had three evaluations to give, which meant a stressful afternoon and a lot of time on the road.

As she headed to the first store, she couldn't help but think about the whole process of giving evaluations.

She knew from her own experience that sitting there in front of someone who presumably had "power" over you talk about your strengths and weaknesses was not particularly fun.

At least from her personal experiences, which never seemed to go very well.

She hated giving evaluations. They always turned into confrontations.

People just didn't like to hear what their "opportunities for improvement" were. And she always got the sense that her managers were staring back at her with a curious look, wondering how someone like her had the audacity to say the things she was saying.

However, the end of the fiscal year was approaching quickly, and she had a deadline to meet. She wondered what would happen to her if she decided to just skip the whole thing altogether.

The afternoon was sure to be a complete struggle. All three evaluations were going to be difficult.

Even though she had given each of the managers the obligatory compliments on their performances, the things "they needed to work on" were sure to set them off in a tirade about a lack of appreciation of their efforts and complaints about "her unrealistic expectations".

At one of her lowest performing stores, she sat in the manager's office and listened to Kent explain away his situation. He complained about how it was impossible to motivate his employees. He had said something to the effect of, "I'm always having to sleep with one eye open with these kids."

Most of the employees, he stated, were "lazy high school kids who were just trying to find a way to fill their pockets so they could spend it all on cigarettes and beer."

She tried to get past all the complaining and tell Kent what she felt that he desperately needed to hear, but she wasn't sure that it had the desired effect.

On her way to her final stop, she received a text message from her boss, Rick. "Cynthia, I have not yet received the profit margin forecast report from you for next quarter. I must have that for the divisional meeting tomorrow at eight a.m.! Please send it to me ASAP!"

Cynthia wanted to scream! *How could I have forgotten about that report?* she said to herself. Her panic almost caused her to swerve off the highway. And, knowing that this information had to be in Rick's hands by tomorrow morning, she had to turn around and head back to her office.

She contemplated how many hours it would take her to compile the information. On the way back to her office, she stopped by a coffee shop, because she knew it was going to be a long night.

After several hours spent pouring through spreadsheets and the previous years' reports, she decided that it would be better for her to head home and work in her home office.

She assumed that the kids would be just about ready to head for bed, and her husband would likely be occupied with studying or working on a project.

But, as she walked through the door into the living room, she saw her fourteen-year-old daughter, Monica, sitting on the couch sobbing uncontrollably. Cynthia let out a heavy sigh.

What now? she thought to herself. She was completely unamused by the universe's sense of humor.

She walked over to the couch and asked Monica what was going on.

Monica, who was still teary-eyed and frantic, said shyly, "Justin told Destiny that Kelly called me a...a...a...I can't even repeat it. Kelly is the most popular girl in school and now everyone is going to think I'm..." Cynthia couldn't make out the rest of Monica's rambling because she was talking into her pillow.

Oh my goodness, Cynthia thought. *Not now. Not today. I just don't have time to deal with another episode of 'I'm a Teenage Drama Queen,'* she thought.

As she patted Monica on the head to comfort her, she continued to think about the huge tasks ahead of her. *Come on! I really don't have time to deal with this right now. I'll spend an hour talking her out of this, and I won't get ANY sleep tonight.*

But her next thought was about Otis and what he had said to service manager at the dealership: "Rejection costs a lot in terms of emotional currency."

She realized that by concentrating on what she had to do that evening, she was rejecting the other urgent issues staring right in the face. Her daughter clearly needed her. She took a deep breath, kicked off her shoes, sat down next to Monica. She brought Monica's head to her shoulder, and began caressing her hair.

After a minute or two she said beginning to reflect on how much Monica was hurting: "You know, honey, I was called awful things like that when I was your age, and I know how much it hurts."

"But... you are so together! How could you have ever been called a...?" Monica asked in a tearful, almost pathetically weak voice.

Cynthia wanted to laugh. *Together*, she thought to herself. *If only!* For forty-five minutes, the two of them talked, laughed and cried together about the pain of being a teenager.

Eventually, Monica, worn out from her emotional catharsis, fell asleep on her mother's chest.

Cynthia would have given anything to do the same. Instead, she shimmied her way out from underneath her daughter, got a blanket and covered her up.

She went upstairs and got into her sweats. She washed her face, made a cup of coffee, yanked out her laptop and began typing in the chair directly opposite the couch.

By this time, Monica had entered a deep sleep and was dead to the world.

As Cynthia looked over at her beautiful emotional mess of a daughter, she couldn't help but smile. *Another teenage crisis averted*, she thought to herself.

She found herself returning to her work with a newfound energy and enthusiasm. It wasn't that the work had suddenly changed into something more entertaining to her.

She just knew that the few minutes she had spent with Monica, making sure that her needs were met, assuring her that her emotional outbursts were normal, and that her awkward teenage phase would soon pass, made *her* feel better.

A few hours later, she again looked over at her daughter with pride. She smiled warmly and yanked out her journal. Then she was inspired to write:

"Law Number Three: The Law of the Agenda

Altering my agenda to align with another's agenda makes me part of the solution and not part of the problem.

Rejecting the agendas of others costs a lot in terms of emotional currency.

Steamrolling the agendas of others is never a good idea.

What seems like a drama to one is a crisis to another!"

Then, she went back to work. She amazed herself when she looked at the clock hanging above the television. She was just about done, and she would have a few hours to sleep before the new day began.

Chapter Ten

Allen's Store

Cynthia had agreed to meet Otis and Allen at the sandwich shop in the northwest corner of Allen's store. After being away on vacation, knowing that he left his store in the hands of the very capable and life-altering style of Otis, he was obviously very curious to hear what Otis was going to tell him.

Allen was excited about this conversation taking place in front of Cynthia.

If fact, Allen thought that Otis would help him make his case for reconfiguring his personnel. In Allen's mind it was actually his employees who were the problem, and some of them "had to go".

When they all sat down at the sandwich shop after ordering, Cynthia took a moment to study Allen.

She had learned a few things about him from Otis, but Otis was very cautious about making "value judgments" about other people.

When it came to initial impressions, she would have difficulty getting anything out of Otis that would fall in the "room for improvement" category.

Still, she was eager for the conversation to ensue. She tried her hardest not to fall prey to her own value judgments as she listened intently.

Allen excitedly began the conversation with Otis. "So the first thing I wanted to say, Otis, is how grateful I am that you were able to take over the store while I was gone. My wife and I were in Florida, and we had a wonderful time. But there were times when I was sitting on the beach and wondering what to do about my store.

"I know that's not the type of thing you're supposed to do while you're on vacation, but I couldn't help myself. I think about it all the time. Some nights I even lose sleep over the fact that I have somehow lost control of everything.

"I wonder about how I am going to keep up with all the paperwork or how I'm going to manage the absences of my lackluster employees.

"So I was surprised to find out that you had completed all of my pending projects when I got back. Actually, I was stunned! Projects that would have taken me weeks to complete were done in the short time you were here.

"I just want to know how you did it. How did you have time to get them all done?"

Otis shrugged his shoulders. Then he said, "Well, you'll be very surprised to learn that it wasn't me who did those projects for you!" Both Cynthia and Allen looked at Otis with shocked looks on their faces.

Cynthia quickly put two and two together. *If Otis didn't do those projects, did that mean he was able to convince one of the other employees to do it?*

"What are you saying, Otis?" Allen said. "How is it possible that everything was done, and yet you claim that you didn't do any of it?"

"The ladies did it!" Otis said proudly.

Allen was surprised by his answer. "You mean to tell me that my employees did everything?" He took a couple moments to collect himself. "That doesn't sound possible, but it appears to be the only logical explanation. How did you get my employees to do that?"

Otis leaned forward, looking into Allen's eyes kindly. Very calmly, but very directly, he stated, "Dude, you don't have any employees. They fired you a long time ago!"

Cynthia, looking at Allen's jaw drop, thought to herself about the ridiculousness of that statement.

Of all the many things that Otis had said to her and others in the last few meetings, that was one thing she could not quite wrap her head around.

She would always fall back to the standard order of things in the company. Rick was her boss, and she was the boss of the managers at her stores. And the employees, who reported directly to their managers, were also under her tutelage.

How is it possible for people under you to fire you? she wondered.

Allen was completely taken aback. "But I don't understand, Otis. They don't have the ability to fire me! Only the DM can do that."

He looked over at Cynthia meekly for any signs of support. She smiled and thought, *Well, he does have a point. Haven't I been saying the same thing since I met Otis?*

Finally, Allen uttered the three words that would confirm his agreement with what Cynthia and the other management team already knew to be true: "*I'm* their boss!"

Otis raised his eyebrows and leaned in further. "Okay," he said, "let's think about that for a minute. If you claim to be their boss, I have to ask you a question: what connection do you have with the people you are the boss of?"

Allen took a moment to think. He visually pictured all of his employees, one by one, and then shook his head in confusion.

"I was promoted three years ago. Before that time, my boss, the manager of my store, was my boss. I always thought of him as my boss. I didn't have the luxury of firing him! He would have turned around and fired me first!

"Then I wouldn't be a manager at this store, and I wouldn't have other people under me who are supposed to do the things I need them to do."

Then, with one defiant pound of his fist on the table, he boldly stated: "I'm their boss. That's that."

Otis started laughing out loud. Cynthia could not believe her ears. *Why would Otis have laughed at Allen like that?* she wondered. *Does Otis really lack the kind of respect we need in this organization?*

Cynthia had come to the conclusion a long time ago that the problem with leadership in some of her stores was a direct result of employees lacking the type of respect necessary to understand the chains of command.

She was sort of afraid to hear what Otis would say next, but she continued to listen with interest.

"They told me that you said to them 'my personal life is private' and that you actually told them that it was 'none of their business,'" Otis said. "Basically, the only connection they have with you is that you all work in the same area."

"I think we'd be on a very slippery slope if I just let everyone I work with into my private life. There has to be a line drawn in the sand; my personal life is my personal life, and my professional life is my professional life. I don't want to get too close to them or I might lose authority," Allen answered very defensively. Cynthia was totally in agreement with Allen, but she didn't make it apparent through her facial expressions.

She didn't want Otis to feel like people who were apparently more in the know were ambushing him. But she wanted to stir the pot just a little bit, so she decided to enter the conversation.

"Wait, can I say something?" Cynthia said, breaking the silence. The air was filled with tension. "As I'm listening to this conversation, I have to say that this all sounds familiar to me. Allen is just expressing something that I have struggled with myself.

"I mean, I'm a district manager. And everyone knows that having authority is important. Clearly, you can't run a store, much less a district, if there is no understanding of the authority I have, or my fellow DMs have, or the store managers have."

"Okay," Otis said. Allen just shook his head in agreement. He was grateful that someone at the table understood where he was coming from.

Cynthia continued, "Everyone knows that you cannot get 'personal lives' all tangled up with 'business lives' or you will lose control over your authority."

"That's exactly what I'm trying to say," Allen said. "I really don't see any way around that."

Otis' eyes had that distant look again. He looked at Allen, maybe right through him, and clasped his hands together.

"You asked me how your projects were finished in the time you were gone. Well, let me tell you an analogy: if a merchant buys apples and sells them all, he can't say, 'I lost my apples!' Right? He, literally, has nothing to lose. You cannot lose what you don't have. Wouldn't you agree?"

"Yes, I suppose..." Allen answered, shuffling uncomfortably in his seat. He understood what was happening, but didn't like that he could see Otis' point.

"Wait, are you telling me that because I didn't have authority with my employees, my projects were taking so long?"

"Exactly! Isn't it fascinating?" Otis' eyes started to sparkle, as Allen just looked at him in disbelief. Otis sat back and asked, "So how's Kendra?"

By then, Cynthia was very interested to see what Allen would say next. She had heard through the grapevine that Allen and Kendra didn't get along very well.

Kendra, who had been working at Allen's store for several years, was constantly questioning Allen's authority—in some cases, flat out undermining it—and Allen had repeatedly sought advice about what to do.

Allen's eyes were shooting flames, as he very gruffly responded, "She's my biggest problem. She won't do anything I tell her to do. In fact, most of the time, she just rolls her eyes like a spoiled teenager."

Otis paused for a moment or two to give Allen a chance to calm down enough to absorb his next sentence.

"But Kendra is the group's big influencer, right? She has been there the longest, knows the most, and has a killer personality.

"Everyone else looks up to her. They *all* look up to and listen to her. When she symbolically fired you a couple months ago, the other employees joined *her* team and at best, give you the occasional forced obedience."

Allen was beside himself with emotion. He reacted to Otis' last statement with a rather desperate-sounding, "Her team? Are you kidding me? How is that even possible? Kendra cannot fire me. *She* works for *me*."

Cynthia took a sip of her Diet Coke and hoped she would not burst out into spontaneous laughter. The passion with which Allen was trying to refuse this idea was kind of funny.

Otis obviously wanted Allen to learn from their conversation. His tone dropped from one of directness to one of concern, as he started to take a different approach.

"Okay, so let me tell you what happened when I was there last week. When it comes to respect, I had no problems with Kendra. She was always very pleasant and agreeable. I think the real difference was that she somehow felt like she was no longer being towered over by some grammar school teacher with a ruler.

"She's smart enough to know that doesn't work! And I know you're smart enough to know that, too."

"But I'm not towering over her with a ruler. That would be sort of cruel," Allen said.

"True. You may not feel that way, but just imagine for a moment that she might see you that way. Even though you think you're doing what you're supposed to be doing, she was lacking the real human connection with you that she really needs.

"As I have said before, people need to feel like they have ownership over their own destinies. Just because they are at work and presumably working for you doesn't mean that they still don't have feelings like any other human being. Before they are workers, they are human beings, and they still have feelings.

"So I took some time to listen to her story."

"Her story?" Allen asked curiously.

"Yes!" Otis said. "So, let me ask you a question. How well do you know Kendra? Did you know that she's working to put herself through law school?"

"Law school?" Allen said. "Well... no, I didn't know that."

"And that's just the tip of the iceberg!" Otis continued. "She grew up in Virginia and graduated with high honors from a very prestigious university. When she moved here, she knew that it would be difficult to work and commute to school every day, but she also knew that it had to be done so that she could pursue her dreams." Cynthia could see the gears slowly turning in Allen's head.

"Dude, she's a natural born leader! As soon as I got her to buy into me, she got the rest of the team to finish all of your projects because she thought I would like that. You need to figure out how you're going to get her to hire you back or you need to start looking for another job."

Allen looked completely lost. The best he seemed to be able to do was weakly mutter, "But...? What...?"

Otis leaned in even further, slowly and softly sharing his thoughts with Allen. "Okay, look, in any group, there is always the big dog on the porch. You get that position by earning it. It's not because you have a title, and it's certainly not because you have the ability to force people to do things they wouldn't willingly do. Authority is earned.

"Now, look at the way you've been wielding power. Are you the one looking at that office of yours, the title you've been given, and then thinking that you have the right to push people around... because you've earned it?

"When Kendra was chosen to be the leader of her peers—and, believe me, it was a choice—she became the dominant player in your environment.

"When you came in, you were like a 'wannabe dictator' because you felt entitled to the ability of telling people what to do. You were voted down, and the troops began rooting for your failure."

Allen shook his head and his eyes grew wider. He was now listening very closely.

"Rooting for my failure?" he asked as if he was reading a novel and couldn't wait for the ending. "Why would they want to root for me to fail?"

Otis continued. "To put it frankly, they like watching you fall on your face. Now, why is that? As for the reason, think about what I just said to you." Allen was too stunned to talk. Otis appeared to be on a roll. He just kept right on talking like a professor teaching a college class.

"It's not rocket science. Didn't you ever wish your boss would get canned because you didn't like the way he or she was treating you? If there were no respect in the relationship between you and your boss, you would be left with very few options.

"You may just grin and bear it, thinking that your job was too important to rock the boat. Or you may start to test your boss. You stop doing what you are told and instead, concentrate on your own agenda."

There's that word 'agenda' again, Cynthia thought. She tried to remember what she had written in her journal about the whole agenda thing, but she was having trouble coming up with the answer.

"Well, essentially, that's what they're doing. That's what Kendra is doing. She gave up on seeing you as anyone with legitimate authority a long time ago. And, once that happened, any attempts you made to regain that authority fell on deaf ears. They took matters into their own hands and fired you themselves.

"Your best bet is to realize authority doesn't come merely because of a title. Your employees are like soldiers. They will follow whomever they believe is the most capable of leading them to greatness. That person carries the most influence over them. Influence comes all tangled up in a whole bunch of concepts like caring more about others than charisma, leadership and yourself.

"If you'll read John C. Maxwell's book *Becoming a Person of Influence*, we can talk again, and maybe start building that future you were hoping for when you got out of college. If you decide not to read the book, I'd suggest working on your resume."

Allen looked at Otis very sternly; he seemed to be wishing he knew what to say.

"I really don't know what to say anymore," Cynthia heard him mutter. "Look, Otis, I know you mean well, but I don't think this is helping. I'm even more confused than I was when I got here."

Otis tried to plead with Allen, but he proceeded to get up from the table. Instead, he got up and just sort of wobbled back to work, leaving a ten-dollar bill on the table and quietly walking way. Cynthia wanted to go comfort him, but she wondered if maybe Otis might be right.

It seemed Allen had always complained about all of his employees. Maybe they weren't the problem after all. She would definitely have to watch this story unfold going forward.

Sensing an air of awkwardness with Allen's exit, Otis turned to Cynthia.

"What he didn't let me say was that I have already talked to Kendra about how he is 'just a guy and doesn't know any better.'

When she realized that I understood that the group saw her as the real leader, she promised to 'take him under her wing' and keep me posted. I'm sure she'll teach him more about influence than any book ever could!"

Cynthia was partially satisfied. He had really thought this through, and he was clear on how to fix what had seemed like a complicated problem just a few minutes earlier.

"It's all about connection, my friend," Otis began. "The Law of the Connection states that the more we treat people as individuals, and get to know them on a heart level, the more they will join our team and create a tribe. History shows that a dedicated tribe is hard to beat!"

Cynthia just kind of stared intently, hanging on his every word, so he continued.

"Allen is just like many other managers out there. He believes that he's not supposed to get too close to his people or he will lose authority. Employees will only go so far for even the best managers. Connected friends, on the other hand, will fight to the death, so to speak."

"But how do you maintain your authority and still be close to your workers?" Cynthia countered.

"I know it seems counterintuitive," Otis explained, "but the person with the most power is the person who only draws his sword when it is absolutely necessary. I never worry about losing authority because the minute something goes wrong, everybody knows who is in charge."

"It's hard to argue with that!" Cynthia agreed.

She began to look forward to the weekend and a chance to replay the events of the week in her mind. She needed a chance to digest it all.

They decided to meet again the following Wednesday at Otis' store.

Chapter Eleven

Company Policy

A *connection, huh?* Cynthia thought to herself as she walked to her car. She tried to ponder more about what that meant. *When I have a heart to heart connection to someone, they usually become a good friend of mine. Is Otis really telling Allen and me that we have to start seeing our employees as friends? There's no way!*

When she tried to come up with a mental list of the people in her life with which she had some sort of heart connection, she could count them all using one hand. *There's Amber from college,* was her first thought.

She and Amber had become instant friends after being forced to work on an out-of-class assignment. They didn't particularly enjoy the class, so most of the time they were together, they would both commiserate about the ridiculous assignments the professor had them do.

They went on outings to the local pizza place and the occasional movie. They would spend a great deal of time together just laughing and ogling college boys.

When it came to friendships, they were perhaps the best example of a heart connection. Cynthia thought that maybe she should call Amber and catch up. She might have some insights about all of this heart connection stuff.

Of course, she also thought about her husband. They had been through some rough spots. Relocating had certainly taken a toll on their marriage. But a new sense of relatedness was starting to emerge, especially after she had posed that very odd question to him a few nights ago.

His college life was flourishing, and he was starting to feel more confident about his abilities. It reflected in every aspect of their home life, and the kids were starting to be more responsive to his more loving personality.

One more stop to make and then on to the weekend... was her next thought. She had arranged her schedule so that after she met with Otis at Allen's store in Altoona, she would then hit Marcia's store in Milltown on her way home. She needed to do their quarterly compliance check.

Cynthia really didn't like to visit the Milltown store. She had no idea why, but for some reason her and Marcia, Milltown's pharmacy manager, were like oil and water.

And, instead of having the happy-go-lucky atmosphere that was always present in Otis's store, Marcia's store seemed more like a scene from a horror movie. She literally cringed every time she set foot in that store. And having to face Marcia made her stomach turn.

Connect? she thought. She really didn't see how she would ever be able to connect with Marcia. They could barely speak without some sort of tension arising. Perhaps there was some one-upmanship brewing between them.

Perhaps Marcia had discovered some way to undermine her authority, and that the true tension between them was because Cynthia was unwilling to listen long enough to Marcia to understand where she was coming from.

In her heart of hearts, she wanted to find a solution. But the most important thing was getting the quarterly compliance report done. She had smartly set things up so it was the last thing on her list for the week.

She settled in for the ninety-minute drive and began to play back the events that happened at Allen's store. The whole concept of employees firing one's boss had blown her away.

Again she wondered, *Why would I be going through all this—traveling hither and yon to these various stores—if people were simply going to "fire" me?*

When she arrived at the Milltown store, she gathered up the compliance paperwork, and prepared herself for a "battle" with Marcia.

But, when she rounded the corner, she immediately knew something was wrong. Marcia was in tears, and she was visibly upset. A chill ran down her spine, and she quickly rushed over to find out what was wrong.

"I just received a call that my son's grandfather Marty was just rushed to the ER and he is unresponsive," Marcia forced out through her tears.

"Oh my! I'm so sorry to hear that about your father-in-law," Cynthia said. Suddenly, all the ill will Cynthia had for Marcia melted away. Just as she had done with her daughter when she was struggling with her emotions, she stopped everything she was doing so that she could comfort Marcia.

In that moment, she saw Marcia as a fellow human being who was really hurting, and not as the enemy she had expected "to face" just a moment ago.

"He's not my father-in-law. My son Jake's father, Nick, and I are not married. But I think of him as my adopted dad.

"My own father walked out when I was five years old, and I haven't heard anything from him since." Then she paused for minute and looked up at Cynthia. "Oh, but you don't want to hear my sob story," she said as she continued to wipe tears from her face.

"Oh, honey, that's okay," Cynthia said in an encouraging tone. "Sometimes you just need to get that stuff out. It'll make you crazy if you don't talk about it."

"Okay," Marcia said reluctantly. "Well, the most important thing is for the ten years Nick and I have been together, Marty has been the father I had always dreamt about. He knows just what to say to make you feel like you're the only person in the world! He has this light that shines so bright. It certainly makes a huge difference to Jake.

He proudly calls him grandpa..." she said. A slight smile flashed across her face as she thought about her darling little boy and his love for Marty.

"Honestly, I don't what we'll do if we lose him. He has supported our family in every way imaginable, and he always does it with a smile on his face."

Cynthia tried hard to process the relationship dynamics Marcia had just described.

Modern families are so complicated sometimes, she thought to herself. While she was inclined to agree that anyone could claim anyone else he or she wants as a family member, it didn't quite sit well with what she knew to be company policy.

If she and Nick are not married, then in the eyes of the company, she and Marty are "just friends."

Her brain raced like crazy. As Marcia's boss, what could she do? Marcia seemed too upset to work. Still, it was Friday afternoon, and she couldn't possibly find a replacement for Marcia on the spur of the moment.

The store was to be open for another five hours and couldn't remain open without a licensed pharmacist present. They hadn't covered this one in management school!

If only it was Marcia's actual father or father-in-law... then I could take the risk of closing the store. I mean, company policy would protect me... right? she frantically thought to herself.

Then a light bulb went off in her head. I know, I'll call my own boss for permission! That's the ticket!

Her mood picked up quickly. She excused herself for a moment while she tried to reach Rick. As she patiently waited for him to pick up the phone, her heart sank when she heard the words: "Hi, you've reached Rick's phone and your call is very important to me..."

She felt as if her head had exploded!! She wanted to do the right thing. She really did. But, she wasn't a risk taker. Time seemed to stand still in her mind. She glanced over at Marcia, who had by then stopped sobbing and was just sitting near the counter trying to keep herself together. She was frozen by how to respond to Marcia.

Suddenly, and for no apparent reason, the question that Otis had asked John earlier that day popped into her mind: "What connection do you have with these people?"

She didn't even have to think about the connection she had with Marcia. She could remember a time in her own life when she was in a similar situation. Her father had been hospitalized just a few days before she and her own family were about to go on a vacation.

The news of his heart failure had shocked the entire family, and Cynthia's mom and her other siblings had flocked to Colorado to be at his side.

Don had tried to convince her that being with her father and the rest of her family was extremely important. They could cancel the vacation and instead head to Colorado so Cynthia could be there. For the better part of a day, she struggled with the decisions she faced.

Finally, she had convinced herself that her father would not miss her absence and that it would be better to just go on the vacation. She thought that she would still have time to visit him once the vacation was over.

But, when she received word that he passed away while she and Don were sitting on a warm California beach, she locked herself in the hotel room for the rest of the week. Don had tried everything he could to get her to warm up, but it was all done in vain.

The thing that really stung for her was the fact that she refused to cancel the trip because the plane tickets were nonrefundable. Those tickets were nonrefundable because of the airline's company policy.

She remembered how frustrated she was when she had explained the circumstances to the travel agent and the travel agent responded by unemotionally stating the cancellation policy followed by the standard, "I'm sorry, but ..."

But she wasn't sorry, Cynthia clearly remembers. *She just wanted to make herself feel better, and her company would have swallowed up my money faster than you could say Alka-Seltzer.*

Cynthia walked over to Marcia and placed a hand on her shoulder. "All right. Tell you what I'm going to do." Marcia blankly waited for a response, but Cynthia simply ran to the back office. "I'll be right back," Cynthia said.

When she returned, she had a piece of white paper and a Sharpie in her hand. Marcia watched as Cynthia placed the paper on the counter and then uncapped the black marker.

Cynthia spelled out the words, "Closed due to family emergency," on the paper and then headed for the pharmacy doors. She walked over to the windows, quickly closed them, and taped the piece of paper to one of them. Then she let out a huge, satisfying sigh. The decision had been made and, for the moment, she felt better.

Marcia was too stunned to say a word. She followed Cynthia to the pharmacy doors. She covered her mouth with his right hand and closed her eyes with appreciation.

Cynthia looked at her with a temporary surge of confidence and said proudly, "Unfortunately, according to company policy, anyone who is not married to an employee is considered a friend—at least, apart from blood relatives.

"Now, I know you just told me that you and Nick aren't married. So that means, according the company, it wouldn't constitute a family emergency if Nick's father is in the hospital."

Marcia continued to look at Cynthia with interest. *But why would you go about closing the store if that is the case?* she wondered.

"Who is the company to define family anyway? You obviously have a very strong connection with Marty, and I could not, for the life of me, get in the way of that. Now, go be with your loved ones! I'll find someone else to work tomorrow!"

"Really?" Marcia said, still processing the shocking news that Cynthia had just conveyed. "I can't believe it! Thank you so much!"

Cynthia thought it was appropriate to share a bit about her own experience with her father. She told Marcia every last detail, and she even started to choke up a bit herself. "I've never quite forgiven myself," Cynthia said. "I would hate to keep you here if it meant you couldn't be with your 'dad' when he really needs you".

Marcia walked over and hugged her, like she had never hugged anyone before. Then Marcia kissed her on the cheek. Finally, she said, "God bless you, Cynthia."

As soon as the pharmacy doors were locked, Marcia took off running for the parking lot.

Cynthia looked at the three support employees who were still on the clock with no place to work, but were smiling with the pride of approval.

She noticed the name tag of one of the employees. "Gary," she said, reading the name tag.

"Yes, ma'am," he uttered.

"Gary, I need you to make sure that the store gets closed properly tonight. Call your main store manager, and let her know what happened. And tell her that I was here and released Marcia to go home.

If you have trouble getting a hold of her, here's my cell," she said as she handed him a business card. "Just call me if you have any questions."

"Okay," Gary said. His expression told Cynthia that he was confused. And his expression turned to more of a concerned look as he noticed tears streaming down her face. "Just keep yourselves busy straightening the shelves or something," and then she quickly exited the store.

She could feel the fear of what she had just done begin to creep into her mind as her adrenaline waned. The last thing she wanted was for Marcia's employees to see her have a panic attack. Her chest was tightening and she felt as though she had lost the ability to breathe.

As she got into her car, she began, very unsuccessfully, to try to steel herself to face whatever the consequences were for violating company policy and closing a pharmacy early.

She returned to the thoughts she was having before she had arrived at the store. Thinking that she was going to have to recover from a confrontation, she thought about grabbing a couple of beers. That would calm her nerves.

But she giggled a bit about that thought, even if the situation at the store was no laughing matter. Her emotions were a mess, but she liked herself a little more than she had when she arrived in Milltown.

She tried to relax. She congratulated herself on another successful workweek. And the fact that she had helped someone in a time of need—no matter what company policy dictated—certainly lifted her spirits. She still had to find somebody to work for Marcia the next day, but she could do that from home.

Ninety minutes later, she was about seven miles from home and she heard her cell phone ding. It dinged with a familiar ring tone. Her heart stopped. It was the ring tone that she had assigned to text messages from Rick.

Her heart sank into her stomach before she could even read the message. She didn't want to look at it, but she couldn't keep herself from pulling over. As she opened the screen she was shocked to see what it said.

"Store manager Kelly called me to tell me what you had done, and explained Marcia's extenuating family circumstances. One of the techs told her how great you were about it. You are a rock star! So proud! Rick. Oh, and P.S., Kelly said to tell you she got a hold of Marcia's partner and he agreed to work tomorrow. Have an awesome weekend."

Cynthia exhaled for the first time in over an hour! *What a relief!* she thought. Not only was she not in trouble for violating company policy, she was congratulated by her boss for a job well done!

During the last few minutes of the drive, she gave herself two or three mental "High Fives" and smiled inside and out.

When she arrived home, she bounced through the door, popped over to the kitchen table, and took out her journal. She cracked open a can of beer. She wasn't quite clear why, but for the first time, she felt as if she was building a plan.

She proudly wrote:

"Law Number Four: The Law of the Connection!

Treat people as individuals, and they will become a tribe.

Company policy doesn't apply to every situation.

Don't get fired by your own employees :)"

Chapter Twelve

The Law of the Appreciation

Cynthia rode the high of Friday evening's "win" right through the weekend. When she told her husband the news, he thought it was the perfect opportunity to celebrate.

Cynthia and Don were able to convince their neighbor to watch the kids on Saturday evening so that they could spend some quality time alone. It had been quite a long time since that happened, and they were fired up and ready for an adventure.

Don and Cynthia held hands as they made their way to the restaurant on Saturday. Don was kind enough to grab a bouquet of flowers earlier in the day, and he surprised her with them just before they would start their "date."

"Oh, honey, you didn't have to do that!" Cynthia said. She still thought that, even though she had literally "saved the day" with Marcia, it was but a small victory.

"Nothing but the best for my little angel!" Don said, wanting desperately for his wife to see how truly special she was. The compliments and loving gestures continued throughout the evening. And then Don mentioned that he had a bit of news of his own.

"Will you just tell me already?" Cynthia said. "You're about to burst into flames over there. I can't remember the last time I saw you with so much... energy."

"My graphic design instructor recommended that I enter one of my projects in the university-wide innovators contest a few weeks ago. He told me that my chances of winning were just as good as anyone else's, but he seemed to think…" he began.

"Go on, honey," Cynthia said in an encouraging tone.

He took a deep breath in and exhaled slowly before he spoke again. "He seemed to think that I would have a good shot at winning this thing."

"Oh, wow," Cynthia said. Don explained a little more about the project, without getting too technical. He always hated when Cynthia was "talking shop," so he was very careful about bringing his school life into their personal space.

But since she was showing interest, and they were in a mood to celebrate, he thought it was a time to sidestep his little rule.

"The first place prize for winning the contest is two thousand dollars. Think about how much something like that could help out our family. We could pay most of our bills for the month, and still have some left over for a rainy day."

"That sounds lovely, dear," Cynthia said. "So, when do you hear about the results?"

"Well, the awards ceremony was last night," Don said. He looked down at the table with a hint of regret on his face. "I was going to tell you about it, but I knew you'd probably have to work."

"Oh, honey. I'm sorry," Cynthia said, not knowing what else to say. For a minute she thought that she was being selfish because her job was talking up so much of her time.

The confident look in her husband's eyes assured her that guilt was not the reaction he was going for.

"Yeah, it would have been nice to go," Don lamented. "But I explained the situation to the panel of judges. I told them that I probably wouldn't be able to attend the ceremony because I needed to be with my family.

"So I was rather surprised when they called me early this morning to tell me that I won first place!"

"What?" Cynthia said with disbelief. "You won first place in a contest you just decided to enter because your instructor recommended it to you?"

"Yep!"

"You won two thousand dollars?" she asked, still desperately trying to process the good news.

"Right again," he said. "They're going to mail the check to me. Should be here next week."

"Honey, that's amazing! I'm so proud of you! Wow, I guess we really did need some time to celebrate!" Cynthia said. She called the waiter over and ordered another round of drinks for her and her husband.

She even let it slip to the waiter that he husband was an award-winning designer and wouldn't he like Don to design something special for him? The waiter looked a little clueless. He uttered a nervous laugh and said, "Okay, I'll be right back with your drinks."

Don stared passionately into Cynthia's eyes. "But that's not what I really wanted to tell you," he said.

"Don't tell me you won another first place prize. This is all too much for one evening!" she said.

"No, no, that's not it," Don began. "I actually wanted to thank you."

"Thank me?" Cynthia asked. "What in the world for?"

"For believing in me. You have more confidence in me than I have in myself. And because you've stood by me, comforted me when I was feeling down, and encouraged me to keep going, I have a new momentum.

"It's like I'm nineteen again. It's very much like I just discovered my purpose in life or something."

Cynthia could do nothing but listen. A tear of joy streamed down her cheek as her glossy eyes met his. She reached out her hand to touch his.

It was at that point when it really started to sink in that Otis wasn't just a fabulous employee—he was nothing short of a miracle worker.

Monday morning brought a tidal wave of emails, challenges, and more tasks to complete. The celebratory nature of the weekend had quickly subsided as she reverted back to her district manager persona.

By Tuesday, she was really looking forward to the next day, when she would meet up with Otis once again. She was eagerly awaiting their meeting at eleven-thirty. As the hours wore on, she was starting to feel a connection to Otis that wasn't apparent before.

The satisfaction she derived from being in his company, listening to his words, and letting his aphorisms sink into her head was truly changing the dialogue in her mind.

She knew that she was nowhere near the level of happiness that Otis appeared to be, but a confidence and determinate continued to grow within her. She had come to rely on his high energy, as well as his ability to live in the moment at any given time.

As she entered his store on Wednesday morning, she felt her energy begin to pick up a little. She wondered what that was about, but she was more interested in soaking up the feeling because she hadn't felt much of that in a very long time.

When she got to the pharmacy, she saw Harvey and several ladies moving about like bees in a hive. Everything was running like clockwork. She marveled at their efficiency, but she also wondered why Otis was nowhere to be found.

JoAnn, one of the employees, greeted Cynthia. "Otis is in the back giving Debbie her yearly evaluation. He said he wouldn't be long, and asked you to please wait for him."

"Will he be in the mood for visitors?" Cynthia asked in a very serious manner. She knew that she was never in the mood for visitors after doing evaluations.

JoAnn thought that to be a rather odd question, but answered back in a very straightforward manner. "Otis? Of course he will! He loves doing evals!

"He considers them a celebration of all we've accomplished throughout the year. He calls it his best chance to share with us how much we mean to the team!"

Cynthia simply couldn't believe what she just heard. *How was it possible for someone to love giving evaluations to someone else?* she wondered. *I guess his version of evaluations is different than mine. I've never walked out of an evaluation where I wanted to do anything else but head straight for my warm bed.*

Without intending to give away her true feeling, she simply uttered, "Oh," and fished her purse for her cell phone. Just then Debbie returned from the back. She looked like she had just won an Academy Award!

Debbie looked at Cynthia and said with a smile, "Oh, hi. You must be Cindy!" she said with a million-dollar smile.

"Yes, I am—" she forced out of her mouth. She thought about correcting Debbie's mispronunciation of her name, but stopped short. *Some other day,* she thought.

"He said to tell you he would be right up! He just had to file my paperwork!"

"So..." Cynthia began, "how was your evaluation?" Cynthia asked with extreme curiosity.

"It was awesome!" Debbie bounced back. "Kinda wish my teachers in school would have been more like 'O.' He really made me feel like I was a valuable part of the team. It wasn't about my performance individually—I mean, we did talk about my personal feelings and such— but he spent more time talking about how all of us work together. It took a lot of pressure off of me. Evals with Otis are always a blast!!"

"I just don't get it," Cynthia said under her breath. *But evals are supposed to be about individual performance, aren't they?* she asked herself. *If that weren't the case, why would Rick spend so much time talking about my approval numbers? Why would I spend so much time talking to managers in my district about their numbers?*

When she was starting to descend deeper into her own web of confusion and deception, in walked Otis. He was humming the melody to "One Night in Bangkok."

Otis took a look at a computer screen behind the front counter, then he looked at Harvey and said, "Harv, it looks like you've got everything nailed down here. Okay if I take Cindy to lunch?"

"Right on, O!" Harvey hollered back. Then he began singing "One Night in Bangkok" to *himself* with a big toothy smile.

"Come on, Cindy, we've gotta boot on outta here before he changes his mind..." Otis called out. He waved Cynthia out the door.

As they walked over to the restaurant in the front of the store, Cynthia kept saying over and over to herself, *Cynthia! My name is Cynthia! Where does he come off calling me Cindy?*

She was becoming a little edgy because she was kind of jealous of his seemingly unlimited energy, and she was just plain upset that he made evaluations fun! *What on earth is he smoking?* she wondered.

Once they sat down and got a menu, she couldn't take it anymore. She had to ask the question that had been brewing inside her. She blurted it out very bluntly.

"Is that why your associate approval rating is so high? I mean because you give out great evals? Did you even give Debbie a list of her 'opportunities for improvement' for the coming year?"

Otis laughed so hard he almost fell off his chair. That did nothing whatsoever to improve Cynthia's mood. But, before he could answer, they both felt the presence of another person.

A nice-looking lady who appeared to be in her early thirties had noticed Otis and desperately wanted to ask him a question. She had a company name tag on that read "Melanie." Underneath her name were the words, "Department Manager."

"Excuse me, 'O.' I hate to interrupt your lunch," Melanie spoke up,

"But, I really need your advice!"

Otis put his hand gently on her forearm and said, "Sure, Mel. You know I'm always here for you! By the way, this is Cindy, she's gonna be joining our team in a few weeks. Cindy, this is Mel; she's the bright young star who runs the housewares department."

Cynthia steamed to herself, *Joining our team? BAH! He makes it sound like I'll be working for him! BAH!* Even thought she had heard similar statements from him before, she decided that it was time to set the record straight.

"Hi, Melanie. My name is Cynthia, and I'll be *his* district manager starting next month."

Melanie let out an obvious, but unconscious, frown in response to Cynthia's statement. Cynthia would have liked to take it back, or to disappear altogether for that matter.

It sounded lousy even to her, but she thought it was better to correct Otis before he started peddling other half-truths.

Otis, however, was so focused on Melanie that he didn't even seem to notice Cynthia's remark. "Tell me, my friend, what's going on? How can I help?" he asked with genuine concern in his voice.

"Well, I've been struggling with something for a long time now. The people in my department hate me! What is up with that? It doesn't make much sense to me. I'm a nice enough girl, aren't I?"

"Of course you are!" Otis confirmed. Once again, Cynthia returned to her thoughts. A statement like that was sure to strike a chord with her, especially since she had been struggling with the same thing for as long as she could remember.

"Oh, you're just being nice," Melanie said. "If everyone thought that way, I wouldn't be in this mess.

"But seriously, I took over housewares like eight weeks ago, and I cannot get anyone to back my programs to save my life!"

Cynthia just nodded her head. *I wonder what he's going to say now,* she thought. *I'm sure he would say the same thing to me if I told him about my "connection" problem.*

"Tell me, my friend," Otis said, looking her right in the eyes, "When you 'took over' the department, did you come in as a helpful observer or as the new boss?"

The deer was definitely "caught in the headlights."

"Did you ask what their concerns were? Did you ask what you could do for them? Did you give them a chance to share their frustrations with you?"

"Well," Melanie began, "I can't say that I did. No, I certainly didn't do that. I came in and diagnosed what their opportunities were, and I told them what I need them to fix. I thought that's what I was supposed to do.

"But, when I look at you, I have the feeling you're going to tell me something very different," she said to Otis. Again Cynthia's eyes grew wide with anticipation.

"Translation," Otis stated. "I came in and completely disrupted their environment... with my own *agenda*. I showed them that I am a problem and not a solution. Now, I am surprised that they are not thanking me for my awesome wisdom."

Both Melanie and Cynthia recoiled. Otis knew that he had hit a very sensitive nerve. Otis gave Cynthia a conspiratorial wink, as if to say, "Watch this."

"Okay, I think I understand where you coming from, Mel. And I'm sorry if what I just send offended you slightly. But I really needed to hammer in the point."

"Which is?" she asked.

"You're setting yourself up for disaster if you just come into a new setting and think that you can wave a magic wand and, suddenly, all of your worker bees are just going to fall in line."

"Hmm," Melanie said. "Okay."

"So let me ask you something," Otis said. "When your husband comes home, does he ever start disrupting your environment without even asking how your day is going?"

Melanie jumped all over that. "Umm, are you kidding me? He does that all of the time! In fact, I can't remember a time when he hasn't done that.

"Just last night, he came home late after a very stressful day at the office. I don't pretend to know what he does all day, but he's very serious about his job.

"Anyway, when he came home, he turned down my music, and immediately started complaining about the bikes in the driveway!"

"How did that make you feel?" Otis asked, listening very intently.

"I wanted to punch him! I was in a great mood, and he wrecked it," Mel said with fire in her eyes.

"Your staff is mainly comprised of women. Is it not?" Otis asked. Cynthia leaned in to see where he was going with that.

"Uh huh," Mel answered softly with a question mark on her face.

"Congratulations!!" Otis said, "You've just become their husband!" Cynthia almost spit out the water she had sipped out of her plastic tumbler. She hadn't seen that coming.

Mel, on the other hand, slapped Otis on the shoulder. She put her thumb and forefinger in the shape of a gun, pointed it at her own temple, pulled the trigger, and smiled. "Ah," she cried. "Okay, I get it now." As she walked away, she thanked Otis for the insights, and then waved goodbye to Cynthia. She knew what she had to do going forward. "Why had I not seen it before?" she said, her voice trailing as she left the table.

Otis turned to Cynthia and picked up right where they had left off. "So, what do you think?" he asked her.

"What do I think? Gosh, I don't know," she uttered. She knew that

Otis would not be satisfied with that sort of answer, so she continued, even if she didn't think she had the right answer to his question.

"Melanie obviously had an epiphany. She suddenly realized that she was being disruptive?"

"Well, yes, that's what she was able to understand. But did this make sense to you? Sound familiar?" he asked.

"Sorta," Cynthia said. "I mean, I can see how her husband was disrupting her way of life, and I can see how that could upset her. And I can also see how being 'her husband' while at work would cause all sorts of problems with her employees. I guess it's easy to see why they might hate her."

At the same time, she was fishing her brain, thinking about how she might even be acting as a disrupter while she is working.

"You asked me if I rigged the evals, I believe," Otis said, changing the subject slightly. Cynthia didn't think that was exactly how she put it, but it was what she meant, so she slowly nodded and gave Otis an awkward, crooked smile.

"As for Debbie's 'areas of opportunities,' we take care of those as they come up in a very caring, supportive, and tactful way. Yearly evaluations are for celebrating an employee's accomplishments and to thank them for giving an entire year of their lives to the company—and to me, for that matter.

"People work very hard all year long. The last thing a great leader does is say, 'Thanks but no thanks. You'll have to try harder next year!' Besides being extremely disengaging, it's just plain rude!" Otis finished with passion oozing from every pore of his body.

"But, if you rate the employee too high," Cynthia debated, "They won't think they have any room for improvement. Isn't that our job? To make them see what areas they need to improve in?"

"What... a... lousy... story!" Otis said, making sure that his trailing words had the dramatic effect he desired. Cynthia had certainly heard that very sentence a few times by then, but was she any closer to fully understanding what Otis meant?

"If you really think that is true, try asking people who don't report to you what their opinion is. Here's what they are going to tell you: When someone rates them low just to squeeze more lifeblood from them, it makes them say to themselves, 'No matter what I do, she is never satisfied! Why bother?'

"But, if you rate someone fairly, or even with a bit of *encouragement*, giving them the benefit of the doubt, they say to themselves, 'Wow! She really appreciates me and my efforts! I'm really going to go *out of my way* next year to show her what I can do!' "

"But, gosh, Otis," Cynthia confided, "I often get pressure from above when I rate somebody 'too high' to 'adjust scores down' to 'leave room for improvement.' What would you do then?" she asked, knowing full well that she may need to have that very conversation with him after the beginning of the new fiscal year.

Otis laughed and said the last time that happened was with a store supervisor named Thomas. "I oversee the pharmacy, but Thomas oversees the overall store budget, and he likes to keep raises low," he began.

"After I had written an evaluation for one of my MVPs, a woman named China, Thomas called me into his office. 'I see you rated China a 5/5 for this past year,' he said. 'I'm gonna need you to adjust that.' I couldn't help but laugh. In fact, I laughed really hard."

"Okay, wait..." Cynthia said. "You laughed at your supervisor because he asked you to adjust an employee's scores?"

"Yeah, I did. Thomas was completely unamused. You see, he's the type of fellow that is used to getting his own way through bluntness and intimidation. But I don't consider bully tactics to have any place in a true leader's répertoire.

"So, I simply smiled and said calmly, 'I would, but there weren't any options higher than five! Is there anything else I can do for you?' He began to straighten up and puff out his chest, as if this was going to become a confrontation.

"Of course, I would never allow it to get that far. But I did need to serve notice that my integrity was not negotiable.

"A few years earlier, I might have acquiesced. In fact, one time I had 'adjusted' an evaluation due to pressure from above. Her name was Brenda. I remember the look in her eyes as she signed her evaluation.

We both knew that it wasn't the rating she actually deserved. I'd love to have that one back. Needless to say, that will never happen again!"

Cynthia was overwhelmed, and she felt like she had just been "put on notice."

Otis lowered his tone and then looked her in the eyes and calmly said: "My friend, it's all very similar to Mel's problem. The Law of the Appreciation says that when we fail to *en*courage, we *dis*courage. Mel wasn't appreciating her new team's concerns, wisdom, and experience, and consequently they vetoed her!

"We really have to give people more credit than we're accustomed to doing. You remember the Golden Rule?"

"Treat others as you'd like to be treated," Cynthia said, repeating the phrase verbatim from one of the many lectures her mother had given her when she was very young.

"Right," Otis said. "So when we give someone an unfair evaluation—thinking that it will somehow motivate them to be better at their jobs—we are actually doing the opposite. It causes the employee to dismiss you as an evaluator! Think about that for a minute!

"When that happens, you lose any ability to influence them. You create an environment of mistrust, and they begin engineering your failure!"

With that, lunch was over and Cynthia was exhausted. She had a lot to think about. What Otis had said sounded logical, but it ran contrary to everything she had been taught about managing others.

Chapter Thirteen

The Washing Machine

All the way home, Cynthia played back the whole scene with Otis and Melanie in her head.

He was so passionate in his thinking, so eloquent in his dissertation. Still, Cynthia was not a fan of change, and almost everything he had said ran contrary to everything she had previously been taught.

Still, there was some part of her that really believed Otis had a point. He was clearly making great strides with his own employees, as well with other people who flocked to him like a prophet to seek counsel for their problems.

He had done extensive research on the topic of how the minds of successful thinkers and influential leaders actually work, and he was telling her things that she never learned while she was going through her management training.

She had to admit, there he was, successfully living life as he prescribed and he was enjoying every minute of it.

As she walked into her house, another matter instantly grabbed her attention. The washing machine was making a noise as if it were at the starting line of the Indianapolis 500 and it was poised to win the race.

As she walked around the corner of the kitchen into the laundry room, she saw something she had never seen before. The washing machine was literally doing the jitterbug. It was traveling in terms of inches per second, and it appeared to have rabies.

Foam was pouring out of the lid at an alarming rate!

Shock? Disbelief? Amazement? She wasn't sure what she felt, but she knew she was not happy with whoever was responsible.

Fortunately, before she had time to verbalize her disapproval, she felt a tug on her dress and she turned around to see her seven-year-old, Jared, standing there in his underwear, with no shirt on, and a hat made of soapsuds.

All the frustration in her face slowly melted. She smiled because of how cute he looked, but she was still thinking about how to deal with "the washing machine bandit."

"Jared, honey, why do you have soapsuds all over your head? Where's Daddy?"

"Mommy, I'm helping you do laundry!"

Cynthia almost fainted dead away. She had not suspected Jared, and she had a couple of very serious questions to ask. The answers to those questions held somebody's life in the balance.

"Okay, where's Daddy?" she asked again, slowly and calmly, with a tone of voice befitting of the Wicked Witch of the West.

"Daddy went next door to help Mrs. Thompson with her sink," Jared said as if nothing was wrong. "He said he would be right back. He told me that you would be coming home. And you are here now!"

If he went next door and left a seven-year-old home alone, he'll be dead before he makes it back up the driveway! she thought to herself.

"Where's Monica?" she asked in low growling voice.

"Oh, she's upstairs talking on the phone. She's talking to some boy, I think," Jared said in an innocent seven-year-old voice. He had no idea how much hot water he had just landed his big sister in.

Cynthia noticed that the washing machine had entered the final spin cycle, and was now doing the Charleston. Even though there was water everywhere, she figured her best bet was to let it finish.

Hopefully, it would spin some of the water out of whatever she might find when she lifted the lid.

Besides, for the moment, she had bigger fish to fry. She had to go find Monica for her sentencing! Just like in the cartoons, a tombstone with the letters RIP popped into her imagination.

But as she began to ascend up the stairs, a different image entered her mind. The image of an almost naked seven-year-old wearing a hat made of soapsuds popped into her head.

She replayed what he had said to her: "Mommy, I'm helping you do laundry!" That caused her to pause on the stairs. She sat down on a stair close to the second floor, just a few steps from Monica's bedroom.

Cynthia could even hear her teenage daughter laughing and joking with some boy her mother didn't know. Suddenly, she found herself laughing out loud!

What was it Melanie had done earlier that day? she asked herself. *She had taken her forefinger and her thumb and formed a gun.* Cynthia smiled, did the same thing, pointed at her own temple, and "fired."

It all made sense now. Her seven-year-old had "helped" more than he might have planned. He thought he was doing laundry for his mother, but what he actually did was force Cynthia to think a bit more before flying off the handle. She needed to recognize his efforts.

She walked back down to the laundry room. Jared was still standing there, patiently waiting for the washing machine to stop agitating. There was a look of hope in his eyes.

He was thoroughly convinced that his mommy was just going to think he was the best little seven-year-old in the world.

"You're my special little man!" Cynthia said as she entered the laundry room once more. "I really want to thank you for helping while Mommy was at work.

"Next time when you decide to help, could you do Mommy a favor?" she whispered softly.

"What, Mommy?" Jared whispered back.

"Could you have Daddy or Monica measure the soap for you? I'd hate for you to get some in your eyes. Do we have a deal?"

"Sure!" Jared said proudly.

"Wanna play a game?" Cynthia said with a sly smile. "What game, Mommy?" Jared asked excitedly.

"This is a super-fun game called Clean Up the Laundry Room! Now, the object of the game is to see who gets the wettest from all the water and soapsuds around."

"That sounds like fun, Mommy!" Jared shouted with excitement.

"Okay, you ready?" Cynthia asked as she grabbed a few dry towels from the pantry.

"Ready!" Jared shouted. He could barely contain his excitement.

"And... go!" Cynthia started throwing big piles of soapsuds at Jared. He occasionally fired back as he screamed with glee. Occasionally, he would run up to his mother and attempt to splash her to death. She felt like she was seven again.

Just then, Don announced his presence at the front door. He could hear the faint laughs and cheers of someone, even though he couldn't quite tell who exactly it was.

"Jared?" he shouted. "Are you okay?" Don rushed through every room of the house checking to make sure that he was okay.

"I'm in here with Mommy!" Jared shouted amidst more laughing and giggling. Don was clearly not prepared for the sight that greeted him, but he folded his arms and smiled widely. "Oh, you silly guys," he said to his young son and his wife.

Later that night, Cynthia walked into Jared's room and smiled as she watched him sleep. She recalled the fun that they'd had "cleaning up" the laundry room. She sat down in the chair that she used to rock him in, flipped on just enough light, and began to write in her journal:

"Law Number Five: The Law of the Appreciation

When we fail to encourage, we discourage.

Evaluations are for celebrating an employee's accomplishments.

Opportunities should be taken care of as they arise.

Never, ever, become someone's husband! :)"

Chapter Fourteen

The Law of the Student

When Cynthia had originally asked Otis for his help, he had requested that she make sure she come to one of his Saturday intern sessions. She was already familiar with intern sessions, since she had successfully completed internships of her own.

But there was something about the enthusiasm Otis possessed—a very familiar, chipper nature—that urged her to agree to attend his session. He had said that Saturdays were his favorite days because those were the days when he met with pharmacy intern, Andrea.

Cynthia didn't understand why she had to be there. She wasn't an intern. Still, she was required to work one Saturday morning a month, and if Rick (her boss) asked, she could claim that she was "orienting Otis" to her way of doing things.

Don was all set to take the kids fishing at grandma's house. It was the highlight of his father-kids time, and it was something that he hadn't been able to do for quite some time.

But his new enthusiasm had transferred over to his roles as both a husband and father, and it was infectious.

Cynthia certainly wasn't going to get in the way of the progress he was making. In her heart of hearts, she believed it was also helping her in ways she never thought possible.

With Don and the kids occupied until Monday, she would go to the session and then she thought she might do some clothes shopping or something later in the weekend.

She was feeling better about her physical self. A few weeks earlier, after she had discovered the Law of the Story, she had been inspired to examine her physical health.

She started eating healthier foods, and she had even found time to fit in a little exercise. That age-old story she had been telling herself about how she was out of shape and not her ideal weight was slowly replaced with a whole new story: *I live a fantastic and healthy lifestyle, and I do everything I can to take care of my body!*

When she visited her family doctor for a regular check- up, her doctor was shocked to notice that that her health was actually getting better with age.

"If you remember the last time you were here," Dr. Carlson said to her, "I was telling you how you needed to lay off the saturated fats and extra sugars. You were at great risk of having a heart attack in the next few years. I gave you the 'Diet and Exercise' speech."

"Yes, I remember Dr. Carlson," she said with anticipation.

"Well, it looks like you've taken my advice! Your arteries look good and your blood pressure is fine. Heck, you're as vibrant as someone half your age!"

"All right!" Cynthia shouted.

"So, I have to ask you," Dr. Carlson continued, "have you been following my recommendations or did you make nice with a genie?"

"I have been following your advice, Doc," she added. "But there's just one more thing that I think had something to do with these awesome numbers."

"Oh?"

"I started telling myself a different story!"

She had quit drinking soda altogether because she learned that she really didn't need the caffeine. She had just been telling herself that she did.

Just by making these few changes, she was amazed at how easily she had lost eleven pounds, and was even more amazed at how much money she had saved by not eating fast foods for lunch every day.

She needed some clothes that weren't falling off of her. Today was her big day to go find some new, slender dresses that would fit her well. She would have fun trying on smaller sizes after the intern session.

Before she knew it, she was excited to head out the door!

When she arrived at the pharmacy, she learned that Otis and Andrea were in one of the conference rooms at the back of the store. They were already hard at work. When she peeked in the conference room window, Otis enthusiastically waved her to come on in.

"Have a seat, Cindy," Otis opened up. "Andie and I are studying one of my all-time favorite books!!" He had a way of shooting past the "Cindy" thing so quickly that she never seemed to know how to correct him!

Somehow, she found herself becoming familiar with his nickname. However, she was hesitant to admit that she was actually starting to like it.

Coming from Otis, someone she was just starting to become comfortable with, it sounded more playful than an attempt at teasing her (that's how she used to think of the name Cindy when she was a child), and that made all the difference.

Cindy it is, she said to herself.

Just as she sat down, a rather distinguished-looking man poked his head in the door and asked politely, "Hey, 'O,' I'm really sorry to bother you, but I can really use your help with something. Can you spare about five or ten minutes?"

Otis popped up and said, "Sure can! Anything for you, my man!" Then he turned toward Andrea. "I'll be back as soon as possible. While I'm gone, can you get Cindy up to speed?" Andrea nodded her head in agreement, and he was gone before she could even answer.

His energy was amazing. Cynthia had never experienced anyone like him. She giggled a little as she remembered watching *The Tigger Movie* with her five-year-old the night before.

"Bouncing around and making people happy is what Tiggers do best!" *Maybe he was Tigger in a past life*, she told herself.

"Okay," Andrea began, "Today we are studying a book called *The 7 Habits of Highly Effective People* by Dr. Stephen Covey. Have you heard of it? It was my homework for last week."

"Homework?" Cynthia asked. "He gives you homework?"

"Oh, yes!" Andrea answered proudly. "He requires me to read one leadership book each week. Then, on Saturday, we sit here and have a discussion about it.

"I'll tell you what, he knows them all backward and forward, so I know I'd better be prepared. I wouldn't want to disappoint him."

Cynthia was astounded. "One a week?" she asked. "How do you feel about that? I mean, that's a lot to expect, in addition to the hours you spend at work.

"Actually, it's not too much. When I think about the fact that the homework is helping me to become a better leader, a more successful thinker—and, by default, a better person—it's probably the best way to spend my free time," Andrea said.

"Hmm," Cynthia said. Of all the times she had been to management training, she was never encouraged or forced or cajoled into reading any leadership books.

She couldn't even remember reading anything of the sort during her entire career!

"So, Andrea," Cynthia continued, "Are you enjoying your intern experience with us?" she added, afraid Otis had raised the bar too high for Andrea.

"Are you kidding?" Andrea replied. "It has been an incredible experience! I'll never forget that first day..." Andrea mused and paused to smile and shake her head.

Cynthia was curious. "First day?" she asked, wondering what he had done to get Andrea so obviously enchanted with his program.

"Well, I was taught in pharmacy school that professionalism was the end all, be all of a pharmacist's existence, right? So, in walks this guy Otis with a Mickey Mouse tie and the most fun attitude. None of my teachers dress like that. And I remember thinking, I sure hope Gina was right."

"Gina?" Cynthia asked.

"Gina is my older sister, and she is one of the pharmacists at the Hometown Pharmacy across the street. I had asked if I could do my internship with her and Al.

She insisted that I would learn more from Otis in a week than she could teach me in a year."

"Really?" Cynthia said, totally shocked by Gina's comment.

"Oh, yeah, Gina says there is simply nothing like talking to Otis. She calls him for advice all of the time!

"So anyway, he walks into our first meeting and says, 'You are probably expecting me to lecture you about side effects, drug interactions, and dosages. That, my friend, is the school's job. My job is to teach you how to build a successful life as a service professional and a leader. But, before I can help you, I need to know what your goals are. Can I please see your goal list?'"

"Goal list?" Cynthia asked. This was just another thing that sounded extremely unfamiliar to her, but she bit her tongue so that she wouldn't keep interrupting.

"Well, I didn't have a goal list. Who has a goal list?" Andrea chuckled. "So he pulls out his goal list and shows me what one looks like. And there, sitting in front of me, was the regular old sheet of paper with a lot of writing on it.

He had the page broken up into three sections, each one having a title.

In the first section he had written 'One Year Goals.'

Underneath he had a list of like twenty things that he wanted to do before the year was up. The next section said 'Five Year Goals,' with more writing underneath it. The last section said 'Ten Year Goals.' You get the picture."

"Uh-huh," Cynthia said. "Go on."

"Then he tells me that my first 'assignment' is to go to the library and work on my goal list for the rest of the day, and that we would get together again when my assignment had been completed."

"Seriously?" Cynthia asked in disbelief. *Who does that?* she couldn't help but wonder.

"Oh, it gets better!" Andrea said. "I was dumbfounded and I asked him, 'What if I cannot think of anything to write?' I really didn't know if I could. Did he really just expect me to plan the next few years of my life by sitting in the library? Do you know what his answer was?"

Cynthia's eyes were wide with curiosity, but she didn't even attempt to guess what Otis would have said. Whatever it was, she thought, it was probably an out-of-the-box statement. She had learned Otis was liable to say anything.

"'Well,' he says slowly, looking right through the back of my eyes, 'Then I guess it has been nice meeting you!'"

"What?" Cynthia's jaw dropped to the floor. She couldn't believe that Otis would just dismiss someone like that. "What did you do then?" she forced out.

"I went to the library and came back with ten goals. I wondered if he would laugh at my goals, but he didn't. Instead, do you know what he did? He helped me write a plan to achieve all of them within the next ten years. I knew then that Gina was right. This is where I belong!"

Cynthia thought hard for moment before she said anything else. She actually remembered doing something similar in elementary school. Her second-grade teacher, Mrs. Sweet, asked everyone in the class to buy a small notebook. In that notebook, the students were told to draw a picture of what they wanted to be when they grew up.

And then, whenever time allowed between lessons, she would tell everyone to take out their notebooks and write stories about being a doctor or fireman or even the president of the United States.

For some reason, Cynthia had been turned on by the idea of becoming a figure skater. She had always loved watching the Olympics, and she thought she would be truly happy if she learned to skate and then learn some moves that would surely wow the judges.

But that dream clearly never became a reality.

Instead, she was looking at a new intern tell her story in the back office of a pharmacy. She let the thoughts of ice dancing trail from her mind as she continued to listen and learn.

"He has you read a book a week?" Cynthia asked. "Don't you think that's a little demanding?"

"It's what he calls the Law of the Student!" Andrea professed. "He always says that effective leaders keep a sharp saw! After this week's homework assignment I know why."

"A sharp saw," Cynthia repeated.

"Yeah. It comes from Stephen Covey. Habit Number Seven is called 'Sharpen the Saw,'" Andrea explained, turning to the appropriate page in Dr. Covey's book to show Cynthia what she had learned.

"I also learned about the Mickey Mouse tie thing this week." Andrea began to teach, although she didn't realize that was what she was doing.

"See here is Habit Number Five: Seek First to Understand, Then to Be Understood."

"Okay," Cynthia said, now suddenly thinking that it might be time to visit the bookstore and pick up this book. She repeated Habit Number Five a few time to make sure that it sunk in.

"Anyone can dress 'professionally,' but almost no one takes the time to focus on being approachable enough to connect with the other person before trying to train them on their medication."

Cynthia was impressed with Andrea's obvious grasp on the content she had been studying, and remarked that she seemed like an excellent student.

"I must admit," Andrea said quietly, "Gina had to help me with Habit Number Five.

"She told me the thing that most impressed her about Otis was his ability to make her feel understood whenever they talked on the phone. She said that he had a rare gift."

"It's not a gift, my friend. It's a skill that anyone can learn!" Otis remarked confidently.

Both ladies jumped as they looked up and noticed him standing in the doorway beaming with pride over Andrea's comments. He appeared to have been there for a while.

"That's why I call it the Law of the Student. Anyone can learn any and all of the skills it takes to get their goal list checked off, but few people will ever be able to do it.

"Why, you ask? It's all about who you decide to become in the process of building your career and, for that matter, your life."

As Otis went to sit down, Cynthia chimed in. "Okay, there is one thing I don't understand. Why did you tell Andrea that you are service professionals? Don't you want to be a health care professional?"

"Great question!" Otis responded enthusiastically. "Andie, I'll give you extra credit if you get this one right!" he said as he looked at the young intern with a smile.

Andrea jumped all over his challenge. "When we studied *How to Become a Person of Influence* by Dr. John C. Maxwell, I learned that you cannot truly impact someone until you **serve** them in a way that builds trust. If I want to help people improve their health, I must begin with a 'Service First' mentality!"

Otis put his hand up to "High Five" Andrea and said with pride, "Slam dunk!"

With that, they moved on to the next book on Andrea's homework list: *The Go-Giver* by Bob Burg and John David Mann.

Cynthia became entranced by the way Otis guided Andrea through a brief summary of the book and his expectations of what she should find once she read it.

"Reading this one will not take nearly as long as the *7 Habits* book did. But I need you to realize that it is no less important. It is an easy book to read, but not necessarily an easy book to master. I want you to spend most of the week thinking through the Five Laws of Stratospheric Success that the book is designed around," he told her.

Andrea promised to become a "Go-Giving Expert" by the following Saturday! Otis cheered her on, and said with a smile in his voice, "I don't doubt that one bit!"

Chapter Fifteen

The Go-Giver

Cynthia's head hurt after the meeting with Otis and Andrea. This guy was starting to intimidate her. She had successfully learned a few key words and phrases from her encounters with Otis, like "service" and "sharpening the saw," but they were all just filling up her head with more confusion.

What's worse, she worried about her future as a "leader" when a hot-shot like Otis was around. She thought about how he might be inclined to second-guess every decision that she made.

She was sure that at some point in the future they would come to exchange not-so-kind words to each other. *But I'll be the one to screw it up and then lose my job,* she admitted to herself.

The most pressing issue on her mind was how she could be successful as his new boss if he was under the impression that he didn't work for her and, rather, worked for his employees. He seemed to be ahead of her at every turn.

She thought back to her conversation with Angela in the car on the way home from her evaluation with Rick. Angela had said that Otis got her "a great eval." That was something she really needed.

Suddenly, going shopping for new clothes had lost its luster.

So she took herself home. At least there, with Don and the kids away, she felt like she could spend some time processing her thoughts.

Before heading for bed, she found herself peering at the bookshelf Don had built in the living room. It was filled with all sorts of treasures from his younger days, as well as a few well-used textbooks from his classes.

She was shocked when her eyes landed on a particular title sitting on the fourth shelf. As she pulled the book off the shelf, she couldn't believe her eyes. It was the same *7 Habits of Highly Effective People* that Andrea was referring to during the intern session. She sat down in a corner chair to read a few pages before falling asleep.

When she woke up the next day, she had one pressing thought in her mind. It was something that she never would have admitted to asking a few weeks ago, but she had gotten to the point where she honored and entertained any thought that had entered her mind.

How can I become more like him? she wondered.

It was indeed the million-dollar question.

What was it he said? Something like, "Anyone can learn any and all of the skills it takes to get their goal list checked off, but few people will do it. It's all about who you decide to become in the process of building your career and, for that matter, your life."

"Anyone can learn. Anyone can learn. Anyone can learn..." she repeated to herself. A smile began to form on her face. The first thing she noticed was a simple thought that crept in unannounced. *But not you!*

"Wait a minute," she said out loud. "Where did that come from?"

She remembered how Otis had said something early on about being able to control his thoughts. He said that he had some way to get rid of the... *Oh, what did he call them?* she said, fishing her brain.

"ANTS! Yes, I remember!" One thing she had always been when she was growing up was a good student. Maybe that was a good place to begin.

She got dressed.

Instead of heading out to the mall, she opted instead for the bookstore. Surely she would be able to learn a few things there, perhaps even pick up some of those books that Andrea was so enthusiastic about.

She wandered over to the business section and began looking through the leadership section.

She quickly became overwhelmed with choices, and she slumped down into one of the reading chairs that was angled across a corner of the store. *Maybe this wasn't such a great idea after all,* she thought to herself.

Suddenly, a broad smile of inspiration came over her face. *Andrea's "homework" assignment! That was it! He said it was an easy book to read.*

Easy sounded like just her speed right about then. But, what was it called? She had seen the cover as Otis handed his copy to Andrea. It wasn't terribly big, and it was bright red. She would know it if she saw it again. *Think, think, think...* she told herself in an encouraging manner.

Just as she was about to concede defeat, she remembered what Andrea had said about becoming a "Go-Giving Expert."

She hustled right over to the information desk and, within a few minutes, she had her very own copy in her hands.

A few minutes later she had a cup of coffee, a very private table in the corner of the store, and she was excited to learn how to become a "Stratospheric Success."

A few minutes into the book she was confused. This was a story. What? It wasn't very textbook-like.

Otis had better know what he's doing! she thought to herself. *I'll give him to the end of this cup of coffee!* she thought.

She still wasn't really sure she believed that the answers to her problems could be found at the bookstore. She wanted to believe that she wasn't the problem.

She really wanted to believe that, but everything she had been learning recently was starting to stand in stark contrast.

She remembered that Allen had "been fired" by his employees for thinking like that. So she kept reading.

By the end of the first chapter, she was hooked. As far as she knew, she was the lead character, Joe. She was struggling, drowning, and desperate...

Before long she was totally engrossed in the story. She began to get excited as Pindar unraveled the mysteries of success to Joe. She wanted to meet, and have a cup of "Rachel's Famous Coffee" with Pindar.

As she continued to read, she began hoping things would work out for Joe. She cried when Joe had spent the night listening to his wife. She laughed when she learned who the "Friday Guest" was, and by the end of her fourth cup of coffee, she was staring at the summary page of the Five Laws of Stratospheric Success.

She wanted to buy a copy of the book for everyone in the store. She wanted to buy a copy for everyone she knew.

Heck, she wanted to buy a copy for just plain everyone!

She looked at her watch and was blown away when she learned what time it was. She had spent three solid hours reading, and it was the best three hours she could remember spending by herself in the longest time.

She knew Otis would still be at work for another half hour or so. So she decided to send him an email:

"Determined to become a Stratospheric Success! Do you have a list of books I should read? If so, could you send it to me sometime? Thanks!"

She pulled out her journal and proudly wrote the words:

"Law Number Six: The Law of the Student

Leaders keep a sharp saw.

Focus on being approachable first and professional second.

Anyone can learn the skills. Few people will."

She flipped to the journal's divider and started a new section entitled, "Book Notes."

Her first entry was the "Five Laws of Stratospheric Success." She heard a blip coming from her phone.

Otis had sent her a document entitled: "Intern Book List" with an attached note that said, "Proud of you!"

She opened the document, took a brief look down the list, and said to herself, *Might have to convince Don to build us another book shelf!*

She slept very well that night as she dreamt about Rachel's Famous Coffee!

Chapter Sixteen

The Law of the Heart

A few weeks later, Cynthia and her family took a road trip to a resort hotel a few hours away. While the kids played in the pool and Don was in his glory on the golf course, Cynthia mainly lounged at the poolside bar and read the first two books on her new reading list: *Goals!* by Brian Tracy and *The 360 Degree Leader* by Dr. John C. Maxwell.

Her husband came come over to check on her periodically; shocked by the amount of reading she had been doing lately.

"You okay, sweetheart?" he asked. "You're poring through those books like the library is going to burn down or something."

"Honey, I'm fine. These books are really food for thought. I think they're really opening my eyes!"

But then, having realized that she was "doing it again," she put down her book and grabbed her husband's hand. "Come on. Let's go for a nice walk along the lake. Just you and me."

"Really?" Don said, surprised by her sudden change of heart.

"Really. That's what vacations are all about, aren't they?" she said.

They spent a few much needed hours falling in love with each other all over again.

Upon returning from vacation, Cynthia drove to Otis' store greatly excited to discuss the principles she had learned, and to get his insights as to how to apply these books.

She hoped he would appreciate her for reading a total of three books since their last meeting. She hadn't previously read three books in the last three years. She was proud of herself! Very proud of herself!!

As Cynthia pulled into the parking lot she saw Otis waiting outside the store. When she pulled up to ask him what was going on, he opened the car door, got it and stated, "Come on, we have someplace very important to be."

She looked at him with surprise. "I don't understand. Aren't you supposed to work this afternoon?"

"Harvey said he would cover me for an hour or two. We need to be somewhere," Otis said with heaviness in his voice.

One nice thing about living in a small town is that everything is only a few blocks away. He asked her to pull out of the parking lot and make a left.

A few minutes later they were at Raushman's Funeral Home.

As they pulled into the parking lot, there were only two other cars in the lot, so she had no real sense of why they were there.

"Do you have some arrangements to make?" she asked with a nervous, awkward tone in her voice. He didn't say anything. He just walked toward the door with a very concerned look on his face.

As they walked into Raushman's, the lobby was empty except for the sound of music coming from the chapel. When they moved over to the door of the chapel, Cynthia noticed a picture of a middle-aged man in the placeholder on the wall. Under the picture, inscribed very plainly, were the words "Richard Jones."

Cynthia cocked her head. She was totally confused.

"Come with me," Otis said, continuing to behave in a very solemn manner. They walked into the chapel and there was Richard, laid out in his coffin and looking fairly handsome for a man in his condition.

Next to the coffin stood two women. One was crying. The other seemed to be comforting her.

As Cynthia looked around the room she felt very uneasy, as there were only three other women there. She would have sworn that they were "rented" as they were showing no emotion at all.

There was, however, an awesome PowerPoint presentation playing on the table next to the man in the coffin. The young lady who had been comforting the other lady at the man's side walked over to Otis and said, "I put that together for Karen."

Cynthia was entranced by the music, the pictures of Karen, their dogs, his motorcycle, and the overwhelming lack of people in the PowerPoint. After five or so minutes, it looped back to the beginning.

Otis introduced Cynthia to Karen and the younger lady, whose name was Kim, and they both thanked her for coming.

A few moments later, a man walked in and said those famous words, "Let's bow our heads in prayer."

After they had paid their respects—even if Cynthia was still clueless as to why they had come to the funeral home—they headed back to the parking lot. It was obvious from the expression on Otis's face that he had known the deceased man well enough to feel sorry about his passing. Apart from that, Otis had continued his role as mysterious and a man of few details.

When she had had enough of the silence, Cynthia gathered enough courage to ask, "Did you know him well?"

"Actually, I didn't now him at all," he said. "At least not until he had already become deathly ill."

"Oh, okay," Cynthia said. "I'm sorry that he passed away."

"Yeah," Otis uttered, feeling a little down. "He had frequented the pharmacy from time to time, but I never really spoke to him until he came to see me after he received his diagnosis," Otis clarified.

"Why would he come to see you then if he didn't know you?" she asked, still trying to process the whole thing.

Otis let out a heavy sigh as he tried to fill in the blanks.

"He told me that a couple months earlier, as a custodian at the college, he had heard that I was giving a lecture to a group of graduating nurses about leading in the new millennium.

Knowing that I had written a book about how successful people think, he was curious to hear what I had to say, so he snuck in.

"He said that he hadn't thought much of my talk at the time, but that after what his doctor had said, he had thought more about it. He began to tear up when he recalled a particular moment of my talk. I mentioned that I had heard a speaker named Brendon Burchard say that at the end of our lives we would all ask three questions: 'Did I live? Did I love? And, did I matter?'"

"At that point, he started to cry. I tried to comfort him and assure him that everything was going to be okay. After a few minutes, he said very coldly that for him that was an incorrect statement.

"'I don't wonder,' he said to me, referring to the answers to the three questions, 'I know the answers, and all three of them are no!'

"He told me that he had not lived, he had not loved, and that he had not mattered.

"But here is the kicker: he told me that he had chosen not to live, not to love, and not to matter. He said he had always blamed everyone else for not connecting with him, not caring about him, and not showing any interest in him.

"He finally understood the backwards thinking that had taken place throughout his years." Otis finished and took a deep sigh that seemed to last half a minute.

"But why did he come to see you?" Cynthia asked politely.

Otis looked up with glossy eyes. "Because he wanted me to continue to teach what I taught that day. He said at the time he thought it was silly, but now Law Number Seven, what I call the Law of the Heart, haunted his every moment," Otis explained.

"The Law of the Heart. I don't think I've heard anything about that one yet," Cynthia said, hoping that she had not missed one of his previous explanations.

What is Law Number Seven about? Cynthia wondered.

"The Law of the Heart says that the more you care about people, the more people you will have to care about."

Otis continued, "He told me that because he had violated Law Number Seven, there would be nobody at his funeral. I had hoped he would be wrong. I mean, how many times do you hear of no one showing up to a funeral? But, I guess..."

"Is that why you came here today? To see if he was right or not?" Cynthia asked, curious to know what Otis was feeling.

"I came here today to mourn the loss. Not of the man, but of the wasted opportunity to live, to love, and to matter," Otis said and took another deep sigh.

He was obviously upset.

Cynthia wasn't sure how to react.

This was the first time since she met Otis that he was not in a hyperactive mood. It was the first time he was not beaming from ear to ear. But, as she was sure to find out, there was a lesson in all of that, too.

He had a sideways frown on his face. He shook his head a couple times and said in a sad voice, "Although, when you think about it, ironically he did matter. He had served as an example of what happens when you break the law."

Cynthia really didn't know what to say, so she just shrugged her shoulders and looked at the pavement.

Otis took another sigh, and sadly looked at Cynthia. "Well, I'm kind of exhausted," he said with a faint laugh.

"But I think you understand where I am coming from here. You don't want to be on your deathbed and wonder if anyone will be attending your funeral. I know it's not something people like to think about all the time but, when you do think about it, it does sort of put things into perspective." He shuffled his feet a little and continued.

"I think we have both learned enough for one day. Would it be okay with you if I walked back to the store alone? I have some roses to stop and smell. I might even stop and have an ice cream cone," he added with a weak smile.

"Oh, of course," Cynthia said with a slight hint of comfort in her voice. For the moment, Cynthia had forgotten all about the books she had read, and she felt like taking a drive. She just kind of nodded and didn't say anything as they walked.

Otis walked her to her car and thanked her for going to Raushman's with her. "I really didn't want to go there alone. I don't like funerals," Otis said.

For the first time Cynthia realized that he was just a man, with real emotions like other men. He was not larger than life. He was just a man who was hurting for a fellow human being who had missed out on life.

As Otis opened the door for her, he noticed the copy of *The 360 Degree Leader* in her back seat. He smiled and quipped. "I love the part where the CEO tells Maxwell that telling his employees that he needed help with his weaknesses is a rotten idea.

"The CEO says that he doesn't want to appear 'weak' to his subordinates. Maxwell tells the guy, 'You're living under the delusion that they don't already know what your weaknesses are.' Genius. Pure genius!"

Otis closed the door for Cynthia, waved good-bye, and began to walk away. She waited until he had made it a little farther down the road before she started the engine and drove away.

Chapter Seventeen

Weaknesses

Cynthia was mortified. She didn't like Maxwell's answer to the CEO when she read it, and she didn't like Maxwell's answer when she heard Otis say it.

Her entire life had been spent in the constant pursuit of perfection.

She had always worked hard at school. And when she started her career, she made sure that she knew everything she needed to know.

It wasn't really a surprise to her that she quickly moved up the ranks into upper-level management.

But with the recent shock of learning that her leadership and "connection" skills really needed a facelift, it was the first time she could remember feeling like an utter failure.

As with other topics of interest, she had worked diligently to fill in the missing pieces. And, with the help of a new character entering her life, she had a shot at making a dent in her weaknesses. She didn't even like the thought of having weaknesses. The thought of her staff members already knowing her weaknesses made her nauseous and a little dizzy.

As she began to pull out of the parking lot, she saw the sign for Raushman's Funeral Home glowing in the distance. That sign haunted her for the next several miles. She wasn't simply driving away from the place. She was trying her best to drive away from the memory of the place.

She didn't want to be like Richard. She didn't want to be sitting in her coffin with no one there to honor the life that she had.

She thought about the Law of the Heart: "The more you care about people, the more people you'll have to care about." And then she thought about the three questions: "Did I live? Did I love? Did I matter?"

The one thing she couldn't get out of her mind was the fact that it was the smallest gathering for a funeral she had ever attended. It didn't matter that she didn't know Richard. It was more important that his belief that no one would come to his future was just about accurate.

She thought it was rather nice of Otis to want to attend and by taking her along, he was surely trying to demonstrate a key philosophy.

You cannot drive faster than your memories and Cynthia grew weary of trying. She decided to stop somewhere for lunch and do some busy work to take her mind off of things.

She was tired of thinking about employee assessment scores, Otis' laws of leadership, who might or might not be at her funeral. Most of all, she was tired of not having enough fun in life.

She was just plain tired! She wanted to go back to being ten again!

Ten was a great age, she remembered fondly. *Jumping rope, playing hopscotch, and no responsibilities*, she thought to herself as she walked into the café she had found in the middle of nowhere.

She scanned the floor of the café and noticed all the strange new faces. As the waitress came to seat her, she sat quietly and just observed the scenes playing out before her. She had had enough of studying and reading and digesting information altogether, but she grew curious about the other people there, just sitting there, enjoying their meal.

More importantly, they were enjoying each other's company.

There was love present between a nice couple sitting at a corner booth. There was obviously a sense of good relatedness among a bunch of high school kids who appeared to be representing some sports team or another.

She had left her phone in the car. For a few minutes she wanted to disappear from the world altogether. *Just for a few minutes,* she told herself.

Her server was a pleasant older lady who exchanged comments about the weather and chitchatted a little about the decor of the café.

Cynthia liked the place. It felt homey to her and she needed that. The old-fashioned antiques made her believe she might just be young again.

She carried herself once again to that simpler time. Even though she didn't believe it would make her feel any better, she did it anyway.

Anything was better than sitting in a pleasant restaurant sulking about problems.

She took herself to the time when her parents had finally bought her a pair of ice skates. In the harsh winters of Colorado, there were plenty of opportunities to go out to the nearby lake and practice those figure skating skills she was sure to master after a few hours of practice.

She giggled slightly as she remembered how she felt when he tied up those laces and tried out her new hobby. Her mom just laughed and waved at the edge of the lake, continuing to encourage her young daughter.

Eventually her memories faded into the present moment, and she resumed her concentration on her life as a mother and wife and district manager.

Oh, well, I might as well sort through the mail while I wait, Cynthia thought to herself as she reached into her bag to pull out the stack that had accumulated during their vacation.

The first couple of items were junk mail that made her feel good to discard. She felt like she was getting something accomplished.

The third item was the quarterly payroll report, which she didn't have the energy or the courage to read; she stuck it deep in her briefcase as she muttered something about the budget being impossible to meet.

The fourth piece of mail was different. The envelope was large and blue and appeared to be an oversize greeting card. *What's this about?* she thought to herself.

It wasn't anywhere near her birthday, and there wasn't any special occasion she could think of.

She never received cards for no reason.

Never!

As she pulled open the envelope, she was taken aback by the beauty of the floral design and the silver embossing.

It looked like a really expensive card. The outside of the card read, "Thank You from the Bottom of My Heart".

The note on the inside of the card brought her to tears:

Dear Cynthia,

The day my son's grandfather (Marty) died, I knew that you were coming to my store to do the quarterly compliance check. That morning, I had typed out my resignation. I was tired of working for someone that I didn't believe cared about anyone but herself.

That night when you came to the store, as you were trying to decide what to do, I was reaching into my bag to pull out that letter to give to you.

I was going to the hospital that night no matter what. When I saw you pick up that black marker and begin to write "CLOSED," I knew that I had misjudged you, and I felt as though we had some sort of strange connection.

I am happy to report that I have since burned that resignation letter.

Thank you for not making me quit! I really do love my customers and the people I work with!!

Your Friend,

Marcia J.

Cynthia was overwhelmed with emotion. She was also overwhelmed with inspiration. It was as if a supernova had gone off in her head!

She thought back through the events of the past several weeks and realized that the first year of being a pharmacy district manager was nothing more than a story.

It was a story that had ups and downs, much like any other story. But, because she had made the story all about her, it was a story that had ended with a thud.

"What a lousy story!" she said out loud as she pounded he fist on the table! The sudden harsh sound did grab the attention of a few of the diners, but then they went right back to enjoying themselves.

"This year's story is gonna rock!" she also said aloud as she pounded her fist on the table again.

The pleasant waitress scurried over to her table and asked, in a very concerned tone of voice. "Is everything all right??"

Cynthia laughed and assured the waitress that for the first time in a long time, things were ten times better than all right.

"Have you ever heard of the Law of the Heart?" she asked teasingly.

She pulled out her journal and smiled her biggest smile.

"No," the waitress said. "But it sounds like it's something I'd really like to know a thing or two about!"

A while later, she walked out of the restaurant, reached into her vehicle and grabbed her phone. Then, she sat sideways on her car's hood. She pulled up her district's pharmacy manager list in her phone directory.

She highlighted the first entry on the list, and then hit the "call" button.

When the person on the other end of the phone answered, Cynthia said with a newfound energy, "Hello, Jen, this is Cindy Meyer. We need to talk. Do you have a moment?"

She looked down at her latest journal entry and smiled at what she had written:

"Law Number Seven: The Law of the Heart

The more I care about people, the more people I'll have to care about.

At the end of my life I will not wonder if I lived, if I loved, and if I mattered.

The people **I work for** already know my weaknesses."

Chapter Eighteen

Rick's Office

Cynthia could not believe how quickly the year had gone by. It was time for her yearly evaluation, and she found herself once again in Rick's office. This year Rick decided he was going to do her evaluation in his office, apart from the other district managers.

She was afraid that this spelled disaster because it may have meant he didn't want to fire her in front of everyone else. She hoped that wasn't the case.

She had grown to love her job and the people who were on her "work team."

Over the last several months, she had taken to heart the many things that Otis had said, as well as the wonderful insights she had learned from her studying.

Because she had saved up plenty of money over the past year, she decided to bring her family with her to the town where Rick's office was, so that they could have an extended weekend vacation at the water park nearby. She had just dropped them off, but she was anxious to rejoin them.

She smiled whenever she thought about them. She now referred to them as her "home team."

She and Don were getting along better than ever, and she was giving him this trip as a graduation present.

She was so proud of how well he was doing at his new job as the IT manager for the entire school district! She was anxious to dazzle him with her new swimsuit.

She weighed the same as she did when she was in college, and she felt great.

She had planned this trip for Don, but she also thought she could use the occasion to also celebrate either her "new numbers" or as the consolation price for "falling flat on her face."

As she nervously entered Rick's office, his demeanor appeared promising. "Come in and sit down, Cynthia," he said enthusiastically.

"If you don't mind, I go by Cindy now. It makes me more approachable!" she said confidently, thinking that her good friend "O" would be proud of her for knowing that.

"Anything for my star player!" Rick began.

Cindy swallowed hard and thought to herself, *Did he just say...?*

"Cindy, I wanted to do your evaluation separate so that your accomplishments for the past year didn't get washed in with everyone else's evaluations!" Rick explained.

"My accomplishments?" Cindy said with the enthusiasm of an eight-year-old eyeing up a Christmas tree.

"Your employee approval scores have risen to eighty-seven percent, and the rest of your numbers look great as well.

"In fact, you look great. I just cannot say enough about the job you've done this year!" Rick said.

"I stopped telling myself lousy stories and started telling myself great stories!" Cindy mused as she beamed with pride.

Inside her head she "High Fived" herself!

Rick loved her new confidence level and was very proud to reward her with an outstanding evaluation.

"Wait until 'O' hears about this!" Cindy said to Rick as she signed the papers acknowledging her contribution to the team.

"I'm just so proud," Rick said, slightly swept away with emotion.

"When he called and gave you the thumbs up, I sure hoped he was right..."

"When *who* called?" Cindy said with a suspicious expression in her eyes.

Rick laughed out loud and said, bobbing his head, "My mentor! By the way, that reminds me, I'm headed over to the bookstore after this to work on sharpening my saw. Care to join me?"

"I'd be delighted," Cindy said with a laugh. "I need something to read by the pool anyway. Do they have a good leadership section?"

Rick nodded and said that they also had an awesome coffee shop there that probably rivaled Rachel's Famous Coffee.

They both laughed and "High Fived" each other as they left to begin the great "Celebration."

The Seven Laws of 21st Century Leadership

1) The Law of the **Contribution**
2) The Law of the **Story**
3) The Law of the **Agenda**
4) The Law of the **Connection**
5) The Law of the **Appreciation**
6) The Law of the **Student**
7) The Law of the **Heart**

The Law of the Contribution

People need to feel important. We are only as important as we make others feel.

People are assets and not expenses.

Make sure everybody contributes, knows what their contributions are, set them up to succeed, and then lavish them in praise and reward them for the part they play in the team's victories!

The Law of the Story

If you want your life to get better, you have to tell yourself a better story!

Any story that begins with "I can't" is a lousy story!

Lousy stories give you ANTS! Yuck!

The Law of the Agenda

Altering our agenda to align with their agenda makes us part of the solution and not part of the problem.

Rejecting the agendas of others costs a lot in terms of emotional currency.

Steamrolling the agendas of others is never a good idea.

What seems like a drama to one, is a crisis to another!

The Law of the Connection

Treat people as individuals and they will become a tribe.

Company policy doesn't apply to every situation.

Don't get fired by your own employees :)

The Law of the Appreciation

When we fail to encourage, we discourage.

Evaluations are for celebrating an employee's accomplishments.

Opportunities should be taken care of as they arise.

Always be an influencer and never be a disruptor!

The Law of the Student

Leaders keep a sharp saw.

Focus on being approachable first, and professional second.

Anyone can learn the skills required to lead and influence others.

Few people will.

The Law of the Heart

The more we care about people, the more people we will have to care about.

At the end of our lives we need not wonder if we lived, if we loved, and if we mattered.

The people we work for already know our weaknesses.

Intern Reading List (from Otis)

1. *7 Habits of Highly Effective People*, by Dr. Stephen Covey
2. *The Go-Giver*, by Bob Burg and John David Mann
3. *The 360-Degree Leader*, by Dr. John C. Maxwell
4. *Goals!*, by Brian Tracy
5. *Pushing To The Front*, by Orison Swett Marden
6. *The Charge*, by Brendon Burchard
7. *The Compound Effect*, by Darren Hardy
8. *Linchpin,* by Seth Godin
9. *How to Win Friends and Influence People*, by Dale Carnegie
10. *Think and Grow Rich,* by Napoleon Hill
11. *Excuses Be Gone,* by Dr. Wayne Dyer
12. *The Alchemist,* by Paulo Coelho

CPSIA information can be obtained at www.ICGtesting.com
Printed in the USA
LVOW01s0117130315

430237LV00007B/8/P

9 781628 651768